today's church

A Community of Exiles and Pilgrims

George W. Webber

ABINGDON

Nashville

TODAY'S CHURCH: A COMMUNITY OF EXILES AND PILGRIMS

261.1X
W386
C.2
8002145

Library of Congress Cataloging in Publication Data

WEBBER, GEORGE W.
Today's church.
    1. Mission of the church. 2. Church and the
world. I. Title.
BV601.8.W396   262'.001   78-32084

ISBN 0-687-42320-1

MANUFACTURED BY THE PARTHENON PRESS AT
NASHVILLE, TENNESSEE, UNITED STATES OF AMERICA

To my colleagues at the
   New York Theological Seminary,
     students, faculty, staff, and
       trustees, as together we seek
         to obey God's call to

"Seek the shalom of the city where I
have sent you into exile, and pray
to the Lord on its behalf, for in its
shalom you will find your shalom."
                                        (Jeremiah 29:7)

contents

preface

After a series of lectures in Richmond, Virginia, I was responding to questions. A man stood up in the back of the room and said, "You have given us a lot of theology and a heavy analysis of the problems of the city, but you haven't told us *anything* about your successes and achievements. What difference has your twenty-five years in East Harlem made?" Almost spontaneously, I responded, "As a matter of fact, the community is much worse than when we began. Morale in the schools is deteriorating, the garbage in the streets is piled higher, the junkies operate with impunity, and tenements are being burned out. The neighborhood is less livable than twenty-five years ago."

I paused for breath. The man stood up again and this time said, "My God, what a tragedy. Twenty-five years of ministry and you have made things worse." I did not share that sense of defeat or failure he felt was appropriate, but ever since that questioning I have been asking myself: "What difference have you made? Or better still, what difference has the church made?" This should be a continuing question for the Christian community, particularly in the face of so many false understandings of success or achievement. When one takes a look at the quality of life in our cities today and at the state of our nation, it is hard to see that the Christian community has had any significant leavening effect. We have not been a light on a hill persuasively demonstrating a new style of life for the people of our time. Yet, for those who read these words, and for millions in our land, there remains a deep commitment to the Jesus way of life and the confidence that God is using his church in ways that are faithful and creative for our times. What is the basis on which one can affirm the integrity of our life and the faithfulness of our commitment?

The question for the church can be asked another way. What is the identity of Christians, and what in the light of their faith commitment is their vocation? These words *vocation* and *identity* point to the twin realities of the life in Christ. Identity refers to our self-understanding, to the basic loyalties and commitments by which we define meaning for our lives. Vocation refers to the implications of that identity in terms of where and how we invest our life's energy, the responsibilities we undertake as individuals and Christian communities. For the Christian, commitment to Jesus is the source and shaper of our identity. Continuing his ministry and mission determines our vocation.

The chapters that follow grow in part out of reflecting on a text that has a special relevance for our day. In Jeremiah are the following words:

> These are the words of the letter which Jeremiah the prophet sent from Jerusalem to the elders of the exiles, and to the priests, the prophets, and all the people, whom Nebuchadnezzar had taken into exile from Jerusalem to Babylon. . . .
>
> It said: "Thus says the Lord of hosts, the God of Israel, to all the exiles whom I have sent into exile from Jerusalem to

Babylon: Build houses and live in them; plant gardens and eat their produce. Take wives and have sons and daughters; take wives for your sons, and give your daughters in marriage, that they may bear sons and daughters; multiply there, and do not decrease. But seek the welfare of the city where I have sent you into exile, and pray to the Lord on its behalf, for in its welfare you will find your welfare."

"For thus says the Lord: When seventy years are completed for Babylon, I will visit you, and I will fulfil to you my promise and bring you back to this place. For I know the plans I have for you, says the Lord, plans for welfare and not for evil, to give you a future and a hope. Then you will call upon me and come and pray to me, and I will hear you. You will seek me and find me." (Jeremiah 29:1-7, 10-13)

I have lived with this text now for several years, preached on it in a variety of situations, and am ever more confident that it is a word of God for our day in a very powerful and unique way. The passage has these specific implications:

Exile is God's doing. The Hebrew people, called out of the nations by God and given a powerful sense of destiny and vocation, clearly were incredulous when told that God had sent them into exile. After all, as his chosen people he had promised to be faithful, no matter what their lapses from responsibility. They had been through periods of punishment and restoration, but the idea that they might actually end up in exile, be taken captive and transported across the desert to an alien Babylon by a powerful political tyrant named Nebuchadnezzar, was more than Israel had been prepared to contemplate. Jeremiah, as tough a prophet as you could find, had tried desperately to warn Israel of her fate if she continued in her affluence, ignoring the face of poverty in her midst, and depending on military might. But all to no avail. As the passage says twice, "I have sent you into exile." It took Israel a long time to get her head around that reality.

Exile had become normative for God's people. In the self-understanding of the Hebrew people exile was now a crucial motif along with that of exodus. How else were they ever to understand that God was not found in a temple in Jerusalem, or that he was not their God alone but was the God of Heaven and Earth, of all creation? In exile they found they could sing the praises of their God in a strange land. He was there, as fully as in Jerusalem.

I suggest that for Christians in an affluent world, in a nation as powerful and self-righteous as the United States, the only rational posture for us must also be one of aliens or exiles. The Christian gospel, in understanding and in responsible action, has to stand in judgment over American society. The Bible talks of interdependence. The world accents competition. Biblical faith accents relationships in which all can succeed. The world strives for might and money. Biblical faith is concerned about God's power. The world agrees when an American general says: "If we continue our faith in God and maintain the biggest air force in the world, we shall have nothing to fear." The biblical world view understands that we are part of nature, called to care for it but not to pollute and destroy it. Yet America as a nation uses up the world's resources at an incredible rate to the deprivation of generations to come and the impoverishment of much of the rest of the world. Yes, Christians should march to the beat of a different drummer. Our identity must be like that of Israel's, standing over against the life-style of Babylon. Christians know that there are realities decisive for the purposefulness and joy of human life other than those affirmed by the media of our time. The New Testament puts it simply: we are in—but not of—the world.

Exile is God's doing, says Jeremiah, and therefore life can continue to have meaning, purpose, and joy. That there can be freedom in bondage is a discovery affirmed by subsequent biblical tradition. So build houses and live in them, plant gardens and eat their produce, continue your family patterns, marry and have children. Don't be afraid to live with confidence in spite of the bondage in which you find yourselves.

The point Jeremiah is making is quite simple. God has shown us how to live. Certainly for Christians, the whole of the New Testament drama of life in community offers a way of surviving with meaning whatever the external circumstances may be. To say that Jesus Christ is Lord is to discover a freedom from the sidelong glance, from dependence on the judgments of this world for our own identity. Rather, we are offered a new sense of liberty as sons and daughters of God.

In exile God's people are also given a clear vocation. If Jeremiah shocked the exiles by telling them that God had sent them into exile, it must have been as great a shock to be told that their task in Babylon was "to seek the welfare of the city." The option was simply to plan an escape, to flee from Nebuchadnezzar back to their homeland. Another might be rebellion, finding ways of making life difficult for the Babylonians, messing up their city. Then there are the more passive responses: sheer apathy like that of those trapped in the inner cities of our country. Denied access to affluence, to the advertised goods and services of American society, the black and poor of our big cities tend to accept their failure as a judgment on themselves and simply drop out of significant participation in political life.

Most of the churches have taken an even more tragic option, uncritically joining the enemy. During the years when I worked in East Harlem, we were often visited by church leaders from Europe or the foreign mission field who had been deeply involved in seeking new patterns for expressing the gospel in situations where the church was very much on the defensive, ignored or opposed by the society. Sir George MacLeod of the Iona Community, after lecturing in a number of large churches in the United States, mostly in our big successful suburban communities, came to East Harlem like a thirsty man to a oasis in the desert. He had never seen anything like the tremendous numbers and success that marked the American churches in the places he had visited. East Harlem, he said, was the only place that felt like home, a place where the church was not "successful" but faced the realities of being in an exile context. "The American churches are truly wonderful," he said. "For the first time in human history, they have been able to overcome the foolishness of the gospel and make it acceptable to everyone. That passage in First Corinthians where Paul talks about the Christ as a stumbling block to Jews and folly to Gentiles (I Corinthians 1:18-25) has simply been taken care of once and for all." This kind of cynicism may be justified. When the church is as acceptable and successful as it has been in the United States since World War II, the question one has to ponder is the whole matter of integrity.

But Jeremiah is offering another option. One does not have to join the enemy. To survive, Jeremiah counsels the people of Israel, "seek the welfare of the city where I have sent you into exile and pray to the Lord on its behalf." As those whose loyalty is transcendent, beyond the claims of the immediate political situation, they are called to function as the loyal opposition, as those seeking the welfare of that place where God has put them. Translate the word "city" into "location." Does it not become the mandate, the vocation for all of us who claim Christ as Lord? Seek the welfare of that place where God has called us in faith and pray to the Lord on its behalf. This is our vocation and commitment.

This preface is not the place for further definition of what this command from Jeremiah requires. But only as we live the vocation do we move from rhetoric to the concreteness essential to integrity. Jeremiah is telling us that we can be free in bondage by freely choosing obedience. In seeking the welfare of the city, in being engaged in this task, whatever the results, we find the freedom that makes life rich.

Thus Jeremiah provides us with the exile motif. I take it to be normative for the Christian life. It reflects our style, our identity, whom we are called to be in our self-understanding. But our vocation is expressed by another biblical motif that runs from the call of Abraham through the whole of the New Testament story: *the pilgrim.* God's people are those who have no fixed resting place. We are not called to build permanent cities, but to be free to follow God's leading in meeting the needs of our brothers and sisters in ways new and flexible and open. Abraham was called from his country to a land he knew not where in order that his descendants might be a blessing to all nations. The prophets were called to put down their ordinary tasks and take up the challenge of God. Whenever God calls men and women to faith, it is because he has work for them to do which disrupts the familiar, traditional patterns of their lives. He gives us an inner freedom that makes us available to serve him. Nowhere is this more obvious than in Jesus' calling of his disciples. God's people are open to what is new, confident in the future, and open to the leading of the Spirit.

Hear Jeremiah again: "For thus says the Lord: "When seventy years are completed for Babylon, I will visit you and I will fulfil to you my promise and bring you back to this place. For I know the plans I have for you, says the Lord, plans for welfare and not for evil, to give you a future and a hope . . .'' (verse 10). So we discover an openness to the future, the confidence that we have a hope that will be realized in God's time. The future is not locked in, but open and challenging. That's why Christians are always young. We never grow old in our expectancy, in our openness to the future, in our freedom to follow the leading of God. In terms of our vocation we are a pilgrim people.

The supreme expression of these two motifs, of exile and pilgrimage, is in the life of Jesus himself. He was an *exile*. The powerful story of his birth in a manger makes it impossible for any ethnic group or people to claim him as their own. Even though born a Jew, he was rejected by his own people and became a man for all peoples. In Jesus, all men and women can find a center of meaning and power transcending ethnic or racial or sexual differences. In him, we become part of a new family, beyond any national family. He lives in the world, yet his loyalty to God transcends all the loyalties of this world. Also, Jesus reflects the *pilgrim* life in his own style. Free of the religious institutions of his own day, he walked the hot, dusty plains of Palestine as one who sought to meet the needs of others, always available to do the will of his father in heaven.

As you can see, this passage in Jeremiah has stimulated in me a whole range of thinking that gives new specificity and shape to my understanding of the nature and task of the Christian community. Our identity is that of exiles in our own land, and our vocation is defined by the freedom of pilgrims called always by a future through which God is beckoning us to new patterns of faithfulness and obedience.

What follows in the chapters of this book is an attempt to give shape to our style of life as a Christian community, as an *exile* people, and then a reflection specifically on what it means to seek the welfare of the city as we fulfill our vocation as *pilgrims*. This is definitely not a book on the inner city. It is a book which considers the perspective which the inner city has brought and applies that perspective to the nature and task of the Christian communities of our country. These are clues for men and women who are called by God, who yearn as I do for a greater faithfulness and a clearer sense of purpose and destiny.

struggle for integrity

"And no one puts new wine into old wineskins; if he does, the new wine will burst the skins and it will be spilled, and the skins will be destroyed. But new wine must be put into fresh wineskins." —Luke 3:37-38

For some thirty years now, ever since the end of World War II, the churches of the United States have struggled to free themselves from traditional forms that are no longer creative for mission and have sought institutional renewal reflecting the integrity of the gospel. For the Roman Catholic Church, this search came to a focus in the events of Vatican II. An overarching concern for renewal has dominated much of the thinking of mainline Protestant denominations. Countless books have urged the recovery of the sense of mission and have offered suggestions toward new vitality. The familiar titles include *The Parish Comes Alive, We Shall Rebuild, A Theology for the Laity, The Church for Others,* and *God's Colony in Man's World.* But in none of them was there any serious recognition that Christians must live as exiles and pilgrims. Renewal books have almost universally assumed that a new commitment to mission was a matter of informed minds and concerned hearts, requiring no radical critique of society. Even the word "renewal" itself implies both a return to a former position of strength and an integrity that can be found by working for it directly. Renewal as such provides an unbiblical starting point for greater faithfulness to the gospel. Jesus reminds us that we find our lives by losing them. In discovering our vocation as pilgrims and our identity as exiles, we may also find at hand the resources our task requires. For those who choose this path, two fundamental axioms are critical. They open the way to an appropriate posture and life style.

Axioms for Exiles and Pilgrims

A. *Iconoclastic about Ecclesiastical Structures.* There are few institutions in our society whose forms and patterns of operation have been as slow to change as those in the church. There is a strong predisposition to believe that ecclesiastical structures as we know them are God-given and eternal. Thus they are not subject to any serious change. Yet the whole history of the church reflects a very different pattern. In each new historical era the attempt to be faithful to the gospel has driven the churches to adopt new ecclesiastical forms and new patterns of life. The resistance of the institution, however, is obvious in the fact that these new patterns and forms have almost always had to be institutionalized in a new denomination. Luther, for example, deeply perplexed in his own soul, was driven back to a new reading of the Scriptures and discovered an insight in relationship to justification by faith which turned his life upside down. Like most reformers he simply sought to call the institution he knew back to its heritage, but the inherent conservatism and rigidity of the institution meant that a new denomination was the only alternative for change. Similarly, John Wesley realized the inability of the Church of England in his day to witness and serve the emerging industrial workers. As a priest of the Church of England, he sought new patterns by which to fulfill the mandate of the gospel. Again the result was being pushed out—and the formation of the Methodist denomination. Again and again in the history of the church a new historical period demanded a fresh response to break old patterns and open up a new way of thinking.

We cannot put new wine into old wineskins. The ever new truth of the gospel demands in each new historical situation appropriate new wineskins if the gospel is to be witnessed and proclaimed with power. Some years ago, I heard Hans Hoekendijk, a brilliant missionary thinker, emphasize that "history is the locus of self-understanding for the church." He was pointing to a fundamental truth. Only as we ask this question in each historical, cultural situation—"How can we here and now be faithful to the gospel?"—thus taking seriously the historical moment, can we find ways of life and expression that will enable God's word to be heard with understanding and power.

But the rigidity of the church is a serious obstacle to any such style. The World Council of Churches coined the phrase "morphological fundamentalism" to indicate the way most Christian communities view their patterns of life as God-given and eternal. I thought of this recently when I worshiped in my home church in Des Moines, Iowa. Since I moved away nearly forty years ago, Des Moines has undergone massive changes. A great throughway has been driven through the center of the city. The Dutch Elm disease has destroyed many of the trees. Many factories have sprung up around the edges of the city. A good part of Des Moines has become unfamiliar and strange; but when I went to church on Sunday morning, it was like going back to my childhood—the same order of worship, the same hymns, the same preaching style I remembered so well. It is no favor to Jesus to maintain such rigidity in an institution which is called to freedom and obedience.

What we are talking about is the "Reformation principle."

Paul Tillich helped greatly by reminding us that it is the nature of institutions to be formed on the basis of a powerful new insight or demand. Then gradually the form of the institution takes over the function and becomes an end in itself. Institutions lose sight of their initial purpose and become self-perpetuating. The "Reformation principle" is the awareness of this tendency and the continual reminder that we must guard and act against capitulating to this switch. In light of the Protestant principle, we are continually critical of our structures, using the criterion of basic purpose, and are not surprised when the wineskins grow old and no longer useful for the task. There are now operating in some governmental circles what are called sunset laws—programs that automatically cease at the end of a given period of time unless they are reinstituted on the basis of their continuing usefulness. Perhaps churches ought to have something like this requiring us regularly to re-examine our worship style, our preaching, our Christian education, and all the other activities in the light of fundamental purpose.

The problem of institutional rigidity and the need for iconoclasm are always with us. The phrase, "Jesus Christ, the same yesterday, today, and forever," continues to be abused to sanction against change: *the church* as an institution, the same yesterday, today, and forever. The uniqueness of Christ is directly related to the freedom he provides us to move beyond tradition in order to follow him with confidence into an uncertain future. Whenever I hear this text used to justify established ecclesiastical structures, I shudder.

A second reason for our rigidity is nostalgia. I find myself on guard everytime I hear a church member say, "But this program worked fine when we were kids." If it once worked and was effective, it must be workable forever! In a world as radically changed as ours, this attitude would seem silly in almost any other institution. A doctor still using practices learned in medical school thirty years ago would be considered a quack. A scientist not continually rethinking the basic categories and processes in his field would soon be out-of-date. Any patterns of the church's life that were effective and powerful thirty years ago ought to be presumed to be dysfunctional unless proved otherwise.

I often get into arguments with clergymen about preaching. Is it still the great center of parish ministry? Can it have the impact it had even one generation ago? In front of the preacher is an emerging generation that by the time it finishes high school will have spent 15,000 hours in front of a TV set and 11,000 hours in classrooms. How could method and style of communication effective thirty years ago be effective in a spectator-oriented, TV-dominated culture? Change, however, need not denigrate the past. Creative change means only that we do not let the ways of church life become idols not subject to criticism and change. A faithful church is a pilgrim church, on the way, traveling light, flexible and free to change ways of worship, organization, study, and action for the sake of the calling of its Lord to witness and service.

B. *Agnosticism about Doctrine.* In this light, we dare not become legalistic about doctrinal formulations. I come from a free-church tradition that believes when Christians gather on Sunday morning for word and sacrament, the Lord will grant us fresh truth. We expect something new to happen. Just as God asks us in Isaiah 43 to forget the things he had done before and to look around to see the new things he is doing, so it is in expectation of new insights and doctrinal formulations that we live out our biblical faith as exiles and pilgrims free to reformulate in our own time and place an appropriate understanding of biblical insights and commitment.

To put it bluntly, I am wary of the phrase "the truths of the Christian faith." My defenses go up against any implication that the meaning of our faith has to do with affirming credal formulations or giving assent to dogma. My commitment is to a human relationship. It is loyalty to Jesus Christ. My creed is this: "Jesus Christ is Lord, and I commit myself to take the consequences of that Lordship in every area of my life." Not a doctrinal statement at all, but a confession of faith and intent? True, but for me, any effort beyond that kind of affirmation to formulate Christian faith is helpful, but always provisional, and only for the here and now. As exiles and pilgrims we have to be free in the face of the new challenges which come to us, recognizing that new theological questions are always being thrown up that drive us back to a living engagement with biblical faith and force us to think new thoughts and to shape new theological formulations.

I will never forget the trauma of graduation from Union Theological Seminary in New York City and being dropped into the East Side slums of New York. Here in this multi-racial and economically poor neighborhood, I discovered urgent issues that demanded understanding and obedience but had never been discussed or considered as part of my theological education. The answers we had been taught did not deal with the questions being asked. This is why every generation in each culture has to write its own theology.

I recall the struggle that Paul Tillich went through in publishing his own three volumes of systematic theology. He found the task almost impossible in a world that was changing as rapidly as ours in the 1940s and 50s. He would deliver one volume of the book as a series of lectures based on detailed outlines. By the time the transcriptions got to him, sometimes six or eight months had passed. He would read the lectures with growing despair, for even in that short time his system had changed. The search for obedience forces the church back ever and again to a living dialogue with scripture. We are not stuck with the formulations of our ancestors, but have the freedom in faith to seek new dogmatic formulations.

Clearly, it is a risky business. We do not create truth for ourselves, nor do we seek to affirm some kind of relativist position in theology and ethics. What a pilgrim faith calls for is the risk of hard thinking and the willingness to live without absolute certainty precisely because we are not God and must always be venturing into situations where we operate with confidence in God, but without the assurance of our own righteousness.

Is it not precisely the task of the theologian to "do theology" at those points where history calls the church to obedience? Our agnosticism about all dogmas frees us from captivity to our own formulations of faith. In our reading of the present historical situation and in interaction with the biblical witness, we dare shape a present understanding of what faith and obedience require. Does this sound like an individual enterprise? Theological formulation is always a communal process as men and women seek together to discover the truth for their own situations. The Holy Spirit speaks through my brothers and sisters more than directly.

In propounding these two axioms, iconoclasm about structures and agnosticism about doctrine, I suggest that Jesus himself provides the central model. The religious leaders of his day saw him as an iconoclast in terms of the forms of Judaism. It was Jesus who allowed his disciples to eat ears of corn on the Sabbath, breaking what was understood to be the meaning of the law. It was Jesus who healed the man with the withered hand and who in countless ways shattered the traditional patterns of Jewish ecclesiastical life. Again, it was Jesus who reinterpreted the traditions of Israel in a way that for his time brought fresh and startling insights to the men and women who heard him. In the concreteness of his own time, in dialogue with the Scriptures that he knew so well, he gave content and shape to the claims of God, calling men and women out of traditional ways of thinking into new freedom and obedience. If our calling as Christians is obedience to him, his style will be ours.

rethinking identity & vocation

In accepting the imperative of mission and adopting the vocation of pilgrims, Christians today find themselves forced to do a good deal of rethinking about the nature of their commitment and the implications. In this chapter I point to four areas where for me substantial reformulation of faith understanding has occurred. My concern is not so much that others accept these redefinitions but that they serve as a paradigm of the task of "doing theology." Exiles in a strange land, pilgrims following their Lord in obedience, must always be open to new structures, new insights, new challenges, however disconcerting and threatening to old ideas and assumptions. In preparing this material, I went back and reread the two books I wrote over a decade ago, *God's Colony in Man's World* and *The Congregation in Mission,* in order to get some perspective on the way in which my own understanding has been reformulated under the pressure of new circumstances and experiences. Here I share four areas where you are challenged to the reformulation of your own faith. I suggest these areas because they do reflect points of strident controversy among Christians today.

From "Taking Christ to the World" to "Joining Him"

By way of confession I recall many speeches in the early days of the East Harlem Protestant Parish which I began like this, "High in the stained glass window at the front of the chapel at Union Theological Seminary were the words, 'Go ye into all the world and preach the gospel to every creature.' Sitting there with several fellow students, we felt a challenge to take the Lord of the church to the pagan streets of East Harlem, where the name of Jesus was only a swear word on the lips of little children." Certainly, East Harlem was a far cry from the lovely chapel on Morningside Heights. But, in retrospect, that assumption that the church possesses its Lord as though in an ark of salvation to be carried around on our shoulders is pretentious and untenable. The fact was that in East Harlem there were many signs of his presence for us to discover. If Jesus Christ is truly Lord, then we are called to point to signs of his presence, to join in his continuing ministry rather than to bring him as a stranger to a world from which until the Christian clergy arrive he is otherwise absent.

The phrase "There is no salvation outside the church," as usually understood, is a demonic misstatement. Looking around East Harlem, we discovered there, amid the problems of that neighborhood, many signs of love and healing and reconciliation. There were occasional teachers who really cared about their children and sought to nurture their potential as human beings. A compassionate store-keeper provided funds for any important community project. So often these people tended to be secular Jews or ex-Roman Catholics; and yet in them, somehow, one saw a spirit of concern for others that reflected the spirit of Jesus. In contrast, the pathetic witness of most of the churches in the neighborhood, primarily concerned about their own

27

survival, serving as a base of escape, and engaged in activities unrelated to the needs and anguish of the community outside, led one deeply to hope that God's presence was more powerful than that expressed only through the feeble instrument of the Christian community. Clearly, God had other hands than ours in New York City. If you take only the people who because of their faith in Jesus Christ are concerned about human problems you have very limited resources to face the principalities and powers that loom so large.

I am not baptizing the secular world. In affirming the uniqueness of Christ, I want to maintain the name of Christian for those who confess that Jesus Christ is Lord and are committed to take the consequences in every area of their lives. At the same time, however, we can affirm the universality of God's grace and the power of Christ, which is not limited by the witness and activities of the churches.

The assumption also that we take Christ to others leads almost inevitably to "colonialism." We who had discovered Jesus at Union Seminary wanted to share him with the less fortunate people in East Harlem. We who had found the meaning of salvation wanted to help those who had still to face the reality of their own sinfulness. There is an almost inevitable over-againstness and an implicit paternalism which says "we want to help the less fortunate" that is inherent in so much of Christian mission and evangelism. In East Harlem, it was a tough problem to determine what we brought that was simply from our middle-class background and what was appropriately Christian. It was hard to take seriously Isaiah 43:18: "Remember not the former things nor consider the things of old. Behold, I am doing a new thing; now it springs forth, do you not perceive it?"

We had been in East Harlem several years before we

realized how little our patterns of ministry, shaped by our own mainline Protestant heritages and by education at seminaries like Union and Yale, suited the requirements of East Harlem. The strength of a unified group ministry supported by outside funds made it possible to exist without any very great dependence on the support and involvement of people in the community. Distressed by the discovery of this fact, we set out to do a better job of communicating and relating. One day we had the bright idea of hiring a young cultural anthropologist to live with the black and Hispanic families in East Harlem in order that she might understand their culture and teach us what we needed to know in order to communicate more effectively. She was hired for a six months' period, but at the end of three months she called together the group ministry, sat us down, and read us the facts of life.

She said she had taken some time off the previous week from examining the community to take a look at the clergy of the parish and discovered what she thought was the answer to our problem. In not very pleasant language she told us that we were "phonies." By this she went on to explain we were playing a very imperialistic role. We were like visitors standing on the banks of a great river watching the swirling torments of life in East Harlem, analyzing, dissecting, giving speeches to suburban women's groups about how the poor people lived, but unwilling to be personally involved or engaged. She told us the only hope was for us to jump into the life of the community, unprotected by our own culture or virtue, and simply share as one human being with other human beings the struggles and torments of life. What she really was telling us was that we had to take D. T. Niles seriously and become "one beggar telling another beggar where to find food." She felt we had been standing in the doorways of our churches throwing life rings out to drowning men without being involved ourselves in the life of the community. She was, of course, simply reminding us of the Incarnation. Just as Jesus left behind the religious institutions of his day and shared fully in the life of the Palestinian world, so Christians have to enter fully into the life of their own communities—not as possessors of their Lord, but as pointers to the Christ who has saved both them and their neighbors. It is the knowledge of this reality which makes the difference, not any kind of new holiness that sets us apart from the common human predicament of sin.

The story of the Last Judgment in Matthew 25 sometimes helps make this point. Those who were the sheep did not recognize they had been obedient, nor did those who were separated out as goats know their own failure. Those who are faithful to the Lord had not set themselves apart as the good guys over against the bad, justifying their faith by the way in which they did good works. I am always perturbed when someone wants to know whether I or someone else has "been saved." The implications of Matthew 25, I would suggest, are that those whom Christ has set free are so busy about their Lord's work they are never preoccupied with the question of their own salvation. Or perhaps like Saint Francis, they remain convinced that the miracle of God is "that he can use even a sinner like me to do his work in the world."

From Prosleytism to Mission

For some years in Protestant circles, a debate has been raging about church growth. A large and thoughtful study institute in Pasadena has stressed the need to emphasize church growth and has sought to share with the Christian world mission the ways in which this can be achieved. In many theological circles there has been considerable disagreement with this emphasis; but recently the mainline denominations, nervous over their failing membership, also began finding ways to place major emphasis upon building up the numbers of the household of faith. For me, the problem can be expressed directly in the difference between the words "witness" and "win." I want very much to share with those around me experiences of meaning and joy, but not with imperialistic motives, not necessarily to persuade them to have my experience or be like me. It is almost impossible, however, to tell Americans that we are to witness to our faith without this quickly being translated into "winning." We live in a world that is filled with huckstering. We are always being sold something. The evangelist Billy Graham years ago was given the award of Salesman of the Year by the National Advertising Club. I suggest that the gospel is not a product to be peddled, but a faith to be believed. Our witness is in the power of a new life, in the style of our commitment, as well as in our words. But we must with great trepidation express the meaning of witness without trespassing over the very thin line into proseletyzing. The opportunity to discover the liberating power of Christ may be forever obscured by the style in which persons are won to membership.

I had lived in East Harlem for several years and had been closely involved with a neighbor. We had marched on picket lines, had struggled for a better parents' group at the local school, and had come to know each other well. I had been too sophisticated to ask him if he had been saved or to try to persuade him immediately to join the church; but I had been operating under the thesis that he, like others in the community, would see the commitment and dedication of my life and sooner or later would want to know why I was the kind of person I am. Then I would be able to tell him that it was because of my commitment to Jesus and all that it meant. This hadn't occurred, so one evening in his kitchen I finally got around to saying, "John, we haven't talked much about this, but I'd like to share with you my Christian faith and what Jesus means to me." To my chagrin he laughed and said something like, "Bill, look at you, white, middle-class, ivy-league, theologically educated. Man, in this kind of world you had it *made* without Jesus. What I want to see are some signs that Jesus makes a difference for a black man like me living in a tenement in East Harlem." My evangelistic strategy went out the window for good. It was not through the meaning of my own life, but through signs of shalom with which he could identify, that this man and others would find a witness that communicated to them the possibilities of a new life and an enriching commitment. The church is simply not out to take scalps or to build up its own institutional membership. We are called to faith because God has work to be done. He will take care of producing the new members for the community of faith.

There is, of course, one striking passage of an evangelistic character at the very first part of the book of Acts. In chapter 2, Peter preaches that remarkable sermon to the crowd gathered at Pentecost. This is often cited to me as an illustration of the need to be about evangelistic preaching with the desire of winning the crowd to Christ. But the passage is in a larger context and is well worth careful examination. Peter does not take a flag and set up shop on a street corner to proclaim Jesus to the passing crowd. Rather, the dramatic event at Pentecost happens. The crowd in Jerusalem is surprised and shocked, upset, curious as a result of the in-breathing of the Holy Spirit in which men heard the disciples speak each in his own tongue. It was this dramatic demonstration of the power of the gospel that demanded some kind of explanation and led the crowd to ask Peter what in heaven's name was going on. It was then that Peter explained in his proclamation what this event was all about. It is also important to notice that at the end he did not make an altar call; rather by the power of God's spirit, the hearts of the crowd were cut to the quick and *they* asked the question "What shall we do?" Then Peter explained that they must be baptized, become part of the fellowship of the church and join those who are on the way as followers of Jesus Christ.

This story out of Acts leads me to suggest a text for our time, namely, "demonstration precedes proclamation." We have the opportunity, perhaps even the right, to witness to the story of Jesus and the meaning of our faith only when the power of that faith has been so demonstrated that out of curiosity, anger, hopefulness, and confusion men and women demand an explanation from us. Then we can relate what we see through the eyes of faith, share our understanding of what God is doing, and make known the power of the Christian community as a sustaining base for our new vocation.

It is a great relief to the clergy when they really can believe they don't have to convert anyone, that the job is to help people to witness to God's love in Christ, to serve, to celebrate, but never to focus on whom God wants to be part of the church. God calls persons to faith. We incorporate them into the body of the church, affirm their new identity, and discipline them for their vocation; but we have no need to worry about the growth of the church. That is God's business, thank God.

From "The Christian Answer" to "Sin Bravely"

A third point of serious reformulation might be defined as the problem of self-righteousness. It is very difficult for me to act unless I am somehow assured that I am right. Just at the point that I arrived at Union Theological Seminary, a group of distinguished professors there published a book called *The Christian Answer*. This only undergirded my assumption that we Christians are those who can discover the ethical answer to issues of race, politics, family life, economics, and all the rest. It is clearly very difficult to live up to the expectations of the Christian answer and even more difficult to convince anyone else, least of all society, to buy into our wisdom. But at least we can operate with the confidence that we know what is right. Self-righteousness is almost inevitable.

Ethical certainty is usually pragmatically impossible. More important, it is alien to the biblical posture. It does not take long involvement in the problems of our world before one discovers how ambiguous is the effort to assume responsibility and to involve oneself in any effective way. In situations of ethical decisions I simply am not God. I do not know what is right and wrong. I do not know the consequences of my action. But a study of the New Testament suggests that the gospel, that is, the good news, which comes to us as we seek to live in this world, is precisely our freedom from legalism, from either having to be clearly right and thus fight holy wars or being immobilized because in the midst of ambiguity we can have no clear sense of direction. Legalism, that is, the confidence that we are right, is never biblical. It runs roughshod over the grace of God. We do not have to be infallible or be convinced that what we do is clearly right to have the courage to go ahead and act.

A phrase is worth a moment's meditation. Luther said, "Sin bravely, love Christ, and sin more bravely still." The danger is in separating the parts of that statement. We are not called to sin with indifference. But having sought as faithfully as we can in the context of Christian community the path of obedience and faithfulness that will express love of neighbor, we go ahead and act knowing we have not been freed from sin by our own righteousness, but only by the righteousness of Christ. I am not arguing for the relativity which is sometimes called "the new morality," but I do accept identification with "situation ethics." People tend very much to confuse these terms. What I am talking about here in terms of Christian responsibility is the necessity of understanding both the situation in which we must act and the perspectives and insights of a biblical faith. That is to say I am not called on to figure out what is the right thing to do from a biblical study and then impose it on the situation in which I must function. My answer in a situation is to take seriously both my faith and the context in which I must act. "In this situation, what is it that faithfulness and concern for neighbor requires?" We cannot know the answer ahead of time. But it is the freedom to live, to act, and to be involved that is the gift of God, that breaks through the Pharisaism that plagues the Christian community.

From Christian Commitment as Status to Vocation

Another area of serious debate that cries out for reformulation is the meaning of *conversion*. Whatever the theology of a particular denomination, almost inevitably those who join one of its congregations follow a model not unlike that of joining a club or other institution. They accept its basic claims and responsibilities, but rarely does this mean a commitment in more than one sector of their lives and loyalties. The church meets persons' spiritual needs, as opposed to the other elements which they take to be important. It has the right to a sector, or piece, of one's time. Biblically, however, the picture is not that of a new status; that is, now one is a Christian or a Methodist or a Baptist.

Rather, in biblical faith, conversion is always to a new vocation. The name was not important for the early church. The calling was. "Come, pick up your cross, and follow me." God calls men and women because he has work for them to do. We are called not to "salvation status" but to "missionary vocation." Israel was not blessed because of its righteousness or goodness, but it was called as a peculiar people in order to be a light to nations. So goes the whole story of faith. God called Abraham to a journey and Moses to lead the people out of bondage in Egypt. From Isaiah in the temple and Jeremiah as a youth to the disciples in the New Testament and to Paul, God's call was to a total commitment in a new identity and a new vocation. In Christ, one is set free to be a Christ to one's neighbor.

A. *Conversion means that the Christian finds self-identity in Christ.* In Jesus, ones sees the meaning of authentic humanity. This is not some different kind of life, but the fullness of life that God intends for all persons. Such images as "from sin to salvation" and "sinner to righteousness" simply distort the reality that is central. To be a person at all requires a personal history, the exercise of one's capacity of self-transcendence and self-awareness. The Christian finds his or her history in Israel, brought to focus in the life, death, and resurrection of Jesus. He is the criteria for decision and action. To put it another way, to be human is to worship, to have an object of ultimate loyalty and devotion. The Christian finds this loyalty in Jesus. The tragedy comes when the decision to make this commitment and to become part of the Christian community is taken to mean achievement of this identity. One has enlisted in the army, but the discipline and nurture of the Christian community which enabled one to grow from the newborn in Christ to a mature person is a lifelong challenge. Contemporary "evangelism" makes so much of the initial decision that the fact that this involves a lifetime committed to achieving the full identity of Christ is neglected.

B. *Conversion means that the Christian exercises his or her political nature as a person for others.* Persons not only must worship to be fully human, but also must live meaningfully in society. Humans are political animals, finding the fullness of life when they take responsibility for the ordering of God's world in politics, economics, government, and the full range of societal structures. For the Christian conversion is acceptance of this political capacity and the expression of it in the ordering of God's world for the sake of all persons. Poverty, civil rights, urban issues, world peace become central items on the agenda to which Christian obedience requires response. We are given a strenuous vocation. However we earn our living, wherever we put down the roots of our lives, to be those set free to do God's business defines our vocation. These are tasks for pilgrims.

C. *Conversion means that the Christian lives as one for whom the kingdom of God is a present reality.* This implies freedom to live fully, freely, and responsibly in God's world, whether this be in slum or in countryside, in east or west, in powerlessness or power. The church supports and sustains this life in freedom for the world, but the society of which a person is a part, the historical setting where one finds oneself, is the locus of self-understanding. To the Christian, Christ has inaugurated the kingdom. Christians live with the confident knowledge that nothing can separate them from God's love. This is the joy of the Christian life. Luther put it his way: "To be the most free lord of all and subject to no one: the most dutiful servant of all and subject to everyone." As exiles, we live in the confidence that the reality of God's kingdom informs us now even as we pray "thy kingdom come."

The Challenge of These Reformulations

As I indicated at the beginning, the point of these four reformulations was both to point to areas which for me personally have been of great importance and significance in recent years and to demonstrate the style of "doing theology." Only as we have the honest freedom to re-examine our theological positions in the light of current issues will we be responsive to God's calling. But this is difficult. Recently in a course on social ethics at the United States Army Chaplaincy School, I was trying to demonstrate the task of "doing theology." President Carter had just announced the so-called "amnesty" for those who had resisted the draft. I asked a group of career chaplains how they would go about thinking through the Christian response to this decision. Before I finished the question, I had two or three vigorous responses denouncing the action and condemning those who had been traitors to their country. I stopped the group to remind them that I hadn't asked what they thought about the problem based on what they had for breakfast, on their previous theological training, or on their locus as military chaplains. Rather, the more basic question had to do with how as Christians they might explore the problem with which President Carter was dealing. What biblical texts would they find helpful? What other experiences in the history of the church could we turn to? What were the issues in American society that related to this problem? The issue, in other words, was not to shoot from the hip in our normal theological style, but to stop and make this a matter of serious reflection that might require even army chaplains, in the light of their ultimate commitment to the Lordship of Jesus Christ, to examine further the implications of this particular action. In a sense, that is what "doing theology" is all about.

"Doing theology" clearly requires the ability to analyze the particular situation in which one finds oneself. Gregory Baum, the brilliant Roman Catholic theologian, several years ago took time out for a serious study of sociology at the New School in New York City, claiming that it was impossible to be a responsible theologian unless one also understood in some serious way areas of contemporary society. But "doing theology" also demands a knowledge of Scripture which is far beyond the resources of most Christians, including professional clergy. In the presence of many of our black clergy, often untrained in theological seminaries, a person like myself often develops a raging inferiority complex. These clergy have taken seriously the whole biblical tradition and bring to it imagination and insight that has made the Scriptures a living sword in their hands, far beyond the resources of most of us who have been trained in our so-called higher critical methods and know a good deal more about how the Bible got written and what the Bible has to say. Henry Kramer has a remarkable phrase: we need again to be "drenched in Scripture." Clearly this is a critical necessity if one is to be about "doing theology."

This suggests that in the future the church will require a discipline of Christian life as demanding as that of any of the sects in order that we might discover and grow in our maturity in Christ. A critical element in this discipline will be the recovery of biblical literacy, a task that, after the initial struggle with any new skill or competency, will turn out to be rewarding and exciting. To the discussion of the Christian community as a basis for discipline and nurture we now turn.

---

life in exile: building the community of faith

Rather, speaking the truth in love, we are to grow up in every way into him who is the head, into Christ, from whom the whole body, joined and knit together by every joint with which it is supplied, when each part is working properly, makes bodily growth and upbuilds itself in love. —Ephesians 4:15-16. Read Ephesians 4:1-8, 11-16.

The striking advice of Jeremiah to the exiles in Babylon was to continue to live life fully. They were to plant gardens and eat their produce, continue the family patterns of giving sons and daughters in marriage that they in turn might have sons and daughters. Life in exile did not have to be a bondage in which the familiar cycles of life were shattered. From the New Testament community, experiencing the reality of becoming outcasts in its own world of Judaism or in the hostile response of the Roman Empire, we also find crucial insight for the church today. Both for Jeremiah and for the New Testament, the critical element in authentic life was the acceptance of a new vocation: to seek the welfare of the city, to take up a cross, to live as a servant. The substance of these challenges will be considered in later chapters. Here the focus is upon the exile community and how it can be a sustaining and empowering base for responsible and meaningful life.

The writers of the New Testament were clearly not very concerned with giving any detailed description of the church. Paul Minear many years ago wrote a book, *Images of the Church in the New Testament*, indicating that nearly a hundred different metaphors or figures of speech are used as analogies or descriptions of Christian community. It is absolutely clear that no one particular ecclesiastical pattern, denominational organization, or congregational style is *the* biblical option. There are, of course, plenty of clues and some very specific descriptions in the New Testament. Paul was always eager to give advice to the congregations which he had helped form, though this rarely related to organizational matters directly. The key scriptures to examine in asking about the nature of the nurturing community into which we are called by our commitment to Christ would include several passages in Acts. In 2:42 the writer indicates that followers of Jesus met daily in one another's homes for breaking of bread, apostolic teaching, fellowship, and prayers. This passage implies that the congregations were *small* and met *regularly*. The four elements mentioned here are worth noting. They are the normative actions in which a community of faith is engaged and whose presence together adequately defines a biblical congregation (cf. Chapter 3). Together they stoked the fires of memory and hope that enabled them to live as an exile community in the face of the hatred of the Jews and the persecution of the Romans.

A second vital passage in found in Acts 4:32-37, where Luke describes in some detail the profoundly communal nature of a community of faith. They had all things in common, having made a covenant with one another so to share. The breaking of this covenant by members brings an immediate and powerful judgment.

This communal and covenantal element in Acts is, of course, reflected profoundly in the ministry of Jesus and his relationship with his disciples. It was the experience of "the twelve together" (title of a book by Ralph Morton, well worth reading again in our time; Iona Community,

Glasgow, 1956) along with their master that is a paradigm for Christian community. Called out by Jesus, it was their experience of life together with him that produced a remarkable community in which all things were held in common and in which they shared a common vocation and identity.

Ephesians 4: A Brief Exegesis

The central passage in the New Testament is Ephesians 4:1-16. Here the author provides us with a brilliant description of the calling of the Christians to a new vocation and then describes the community in which the vocation can be sustained by the achievement of a new identity, the maturity and stature of Christ. This passage has a specificity and directness about it which has to be taken seriously. The authorship of the letter is hotly contested by scholars, but the contents are clearly Pauline in character and emphasis. Here we shall refer to Paul as the author.

Paul begins with a concrete word addressed to each of us, "I therefore, a prisoner for the Lord, beg you to lead a life worthy of the calling to which you have been called." We have been given a new vocation. Each one of us has had hands laid upon us, just as clearly as Moses was called to a task for God or Paul himself was challenged on the Damascus road and then set forth as a messenger for God. Paul then continues with a description of the style of our new life, stressing the unity which is granted to all who follow Christ. Yet he is also fully aware that it is a unity which allows for wide diversity. We have been given different gifts, but because we are now sons and daughters of one father, with one Lord and one baptism, this diversity is not a negative experience that breaks down community but a positive one that enriches community for all. We need to be reminded that when Paul speaks of lowliness, meekness, patience, and forebearance, these are not attitudes which must be expressed with a stiff upper lip or grim determination. They are the natural expressions of a community in which the members genuinely love one another. They are not demands, but inevitable aspects of the fruits of the Spirit. When church members view these expressions as demands and are determined to express them in spite of deep feelings to the contrary, they turn empty or shallow.

The significant part of the chapter for the life of the Christian community comes in verses 11 to 16. Here the author is quite explicit about the goal. We are called to participate in the community in order that we attain the unity of the faith and mature personhood, "the measure of the stature of the fulness of Christ." The congregation is a nurturing community. All of us must recognize that at the point we made a life commitment to Christ we are in faith only one day old. We will need to be involved for the rest of our lives in growing toward maturity and the stature of Christ. When the nurturing process stops and growth in Christ ceases, Christian faith atrophies and the community no longer is faithful.

Note also the important clues as to what makes a community open to the Holy Spirit and hopefully makes the nurturing mission possible.

(1) The acceptance of the gifts guaranteed by the Holy Spirit as possessions to each member of the congregation. Paul clearly is addressing all the members. These gifts are not granted to a particular breed called clergy.

(2) The mutual interdependence symbolized by the fact that bodily growth takes place only when every joint with which the community is supplied is working properly.

(3) Speaking the truth in love. When such loving

---

truthfulness is a reality, then a family is real and the context for growth for all the members is possible.

It is discouraging in light of this passage to reflect upon the various communities of faith one knows in a city like New York. The passage comes initially as a harsh judgment. Imagine using Ephesians to describe the reality and shape of Christian community to someone who was unfamiliar with Christianity. Finally the person says, "I'm tired of just these words. Take me to a community like the one you described so I can see and feel and taste it." I would be hard put to know where to go next Sunday with my visiting friend. Certainly not to one of the massive Gothic structures on one of the avenues where the gathering for the Sunday service is the only common activity of the community and where there is little chance for the intimacy of the family to be found. I would be more likely to go to one of the fine black churches in Harlem or one of the lively pentecostal Hispanic churches, but even here I would be troubled by the fact that these are homogeneous ethnic churches foundering as surely as the white congregations on the Scylla and Charybdis of racism and sexism which shipwreck the integrity of almost every American congregation. Certainly Paul's many letters of admonition to the churches in the New Testament give us no right to idealize any New Testament congregation. But one does have to search pretty hard to find congregations who have discovered the elements of Ephesians 4 and who reflect the openness to the Holy Spirit and to the presence of Christ for which one longs.

Daytop As a Parable

The closest parallel to the pattern in Ephesians that I have discovered is one of the numerous therapeutic communities for drug addicts that have sprung up in recent years. I once spent four days at Daytop, one such center located near New York City, where over many months in a protected environment former addicts are helped to become "new human beings" (their phrase) in a program that has emerged through trial and error, but seems to be a remarkable secular expression of the very insights of Ephesians. The 120 men and women are helped to discover their own unique gifts and are required to speak the truth and gradually to discover the power of truth spoken in love, to accept the mutual interdependence and thus to break old patterns of bondage.

After a forty-hour marathon staged for a group of twelve professionals by three Daytop residents, I was prepared to affirm that Daytop really works. For me it was a tremendously joyous and powerful discovery. As I drove home from Daytop still feeling the power and joy of that experience, I suddenly realized that Daytop was living by the insights of Ephesians 4 in a way that made those verses alive and real. Daytop begins with a profound sense of commitment. Former addicts have been called to a new life out of their bondage to addiction. In the community to which they are called to begin this new life, there is a tremendous diversity which, however, is made creative by the unity which is clearly discovered. They are part of one community to whom their loyalty must be unconditional. They are part of a community of sinners anonymous with a new hope that arises from the search for a new life in maturity. At Daytop, they recognize the variety of gifts which are required. Every member of the community has an assignment which is critical for the welfare of everyone. Daytop really believes that no human being is without gifts which are useful and creative for the whole body and sets about in a very detailed way to discover what its various members have to offer in the way of their human skills and potential. Daytoppers are also well aware of their mutual interdependence. If someone in the community is sick, then everyone feels the pain of it. If someone is breaking the rules, then the whole community has to stop and deal with that problem. They know that unless every part is working properly, it is very difficult for bodily growth to take place and for the community to upbuild itself in love. Finally, Daytop is a place that takes with absolute seriousness the necessity of speaking the truth, hopefully in love. A person who is not absolutely honest in relationships simply is not tolerated by the discipline of the whole community. Perhaps Daytop suspects that you cannot force people to love, but it does believe that being truthful and open in one's own life makes possible the growth of love among men and women in a community. Finally, Daytop is under no illusions about the pain and difficulty which the task requires. For a new human being to emerge out of the broken life of the junkie world is no easy business. It is hard, painful, and demanding; but Daytoppers are willing to pay the price.

Implications for the Congregation

A. *Judgment.* Reflection on Ephesians 4 and on the Daytop parable is likely to produce in most congregations a very strong sense of judgment. The almost inevitable tendency is to downplay the importance of this scripture or to avoid the bite, but let us take as clear a look as we can at the implicit judgment in the confidence that when judgment begins with the household of faith there is also opportunity for redirection and new hope. The judgments come at six very precise points.

1. Commitment as the starting point. To enter the early

Christian community was a very demanding decision. As in all missionary situations, the decision to become an exile from one's own family and community is a terribly painful process. It was no joke to become a Christian in the first or second century. The degree of the commitment was clear. The early disciples were called to leave the familiar patterns of life for the sake of their new vocation. In all ages the exile life of the Christian community may not mean one has to leave one's present situation but always does mean one has to assume a new posture in relationship to the places where it is lived out. But, in any case, to be part of the Christian community is not simply a matter of joining another organization or voting "Yes" for Jesus, but a matter of a willingness to take the consequences of our life.

I was startled to discover how difficult, for example, Daytop makes it for anyone to begin the therapeutic process. It simply has no time for the junkie who, in desperation because he cannot find a fix, decides to go to Daytop in order to dry out long enough to reduce the level of his habit and get his head straight again. The process of initiation into Daytop is a very painful and testing one through which the seriousness of one's commitment is rigorously tested with no ambiguity allowed. It has all the characteristics of the encounter between Jesus and the rich young ruler. Remember the story in which this fine, honest young businessman asked Jesus what he must do to be saved. Jesus gives him very clearly the ground rules for obedience; in this case to indicate his new loyalty he must sell his worldly goods and enter a new style of life. Jesus did not reject the young man. He simply made the condition so unambiguously clear that in sorrow the young man turned away. It is difficult to imagine any congregation hesitating for one moment in encouraging such an outstanding young community leader from joining its ranks. One can imagine that within six months, he would be a key church officer, chairing the every-member canvass. Commitment to a new life is the starting point for the experience of Christian community.

2. Unity and diversity. Ephesians 4 assumes that we have been given a new unity expressed in one hope, one Lord, one faith, one baptism, one God and Father of us all. This does not eliminate human diversity, but makes it more precious. In a sense, Paul is suggesting that because God has called us, we dare see ourselves as useful in the kingdom and thus have a new capacity to love and accept ourselves. That capacity alone makes possible the love of neighbor. At a recent general synod of the United Church of Christ, a brilliant clergyperson called for the recovery of "moral fiber," by which she did not mean the legalism with which we usually associate those terms. She was not calling for the personal sense of righteousness over against the unrighteous, the attitude of so many Christian communities whose energy is spent on judging those who do not maintain the standards of the Christian faith and seek to impose their own patterns upon the secular world. By moral fiber the young preacher meant simply the recovery of my personal sense of self-worth. Such a sense of my own worthiness means I no longer have to stand in judgment over against others, to affirm that I am better than another person. It is the freedom to allow others to be who they are, even as I accept who I am, as a child of God.

The stress here on acceptance is underlined by a passage in Paul's letter to the Galatians. "Bear one another's burden. . . . For each man will have to bear his own load." How apparent it is that in most churches we have created an ethos in which the congregation is expected to bear the burdens of its members rather than the other way around. Joining the church and paying one's dues means a claim on the clergyperson to be the paid burden-bearer of the fellowship. The pastor is there to support and encourage and sustain; the pastor is paid to meet my spiritual needs. Paul turns upside down our normal expectations when he reminds us that we are set free by Christ from our own self-concern and preoccupation now with new freedom to bear the burdens of others. Instead of the church's being seen primarily as a place where I am helped, it is seen as the place where I can find strength, encouragement, and wisdom to bear the burdens of others.

How like a family picture this text becomes. When one member of the family demands that others take care of him or her rather than each seeking to be a burden-bearer for the whole of one's relations, the family is in for trouble. I shudder every time I hear a parent say to a child, "Because I did thus and so for you, you better do this for me." That's a sure sign that a family is falling to pieces. Reflect for a moment on your own congregations. How often do you hear people complaining about the fact that a small group does all the work.

I don't mean to obscure the fact that we need support even as we support others, but I do want to underline the joyous reality of the Christian life. When we have no claim on our brother and sister as any kind of demand, then we are always surprised by the way in which our own burdens are being picked up and sustained by the freely given concern of others. When we do not make a claim on our brothers and sisters, we are always surprised by the gifts of grace which come to us through them. When it is not a demand, there is far greater freedom for the gift to be given.

3. The variety of gifts. In Ephesians, the author writes, "And his gifts were that some should be apostles, some prophets, some evangelists, some pastors and teachers for the equipment of the saints, for the work of ministry, for

building up the body of Christ." Parallel lists appear also in Paul's writings in First Corinthians 12 and in Romans 12. Clearly, this is an important emphasis. It is appalling when these varieties of gifts are taken to be a basic description of the qualities of an ordained clergyperson. Far too often I have heard an ordination sermon in which the young pastor was told to express the qualities of pastor, prophet, teacher, evangelist, and apostle when, in fact, these gifts may be mutually exclusive. Clearly, in Ephesians, as in Corinthians and Romans, we are reminded that all members of the body of Christ are given gifts of the Spirit as well as human competencies that are needed for the health of the whole body. The discovering, empowering, and expressing of these gifts is a primary task for the leadership of a congregation. Certainly it is not the unique possession of a number of the gifts that qualifies one for leadership. Members of the congregation, whatever their age or human qualifications, are important and useful.

Daytop is a good reminder that "professional" training may not be critical for an effective community of nurture. It does seem clear that we have messed up our congregations sadly in making their lives center on the preacher. Our pattern is one of concentric circles. The minister is at the center, surrounded by a group of top lay leaders, usually men. Then there are the hard group of willing workers who teach the Sunday school classes and cook the church suppers and who can be counted on for loyal participation in any events in the church's life. Around them is a circle of those who are faithful in church attendance. Another circle contains those who attend more occasionally but give regularly. Then there is the circle of the Easter/Christmas attenders. Around them is another circle of all those who say, "That's my church." If one takes seriously the implications of Ephesians 4, this model of church life is simply devastating. It fails completely to recognize the need for variety of gifts; but, more important, it points to our next level of judgment.

4. Mutual interdependence. The body only grows when every part which is joined and knit together is working properly. Then growth takes place, and the body will upbuild itself in love. The concentric circle model is an absolute denial of this necessity. The early church discerned a pattern of mutuality, which made possible mutual growth and interdependence. The church was an intentional community, but not in any necessarily sectarian sense. Its purpose was to establish the discipline of a community of nurture and to be an effective base in its pilgrim vocation. This emphasis upon the importance of every part's working properly did not exclude a circle of inquirers who were seeking to relate to the community and were beginning to discover something of the implications of this life, but it meant a clear distinction of those who had taken on the decision of commitment and the consequences of obedience to Christ. It is precisely the model used by the Church of the Savior in Washington, D.C., the most powerful example of an Ephesians 4 community I have encountered in middle-class American Protestantism. Here the cadre of committed members, who make a yearly covenant renewal, may be only 70 or 80. But the participants in the life of the community, those who are sharing in its life and, in most cases, seeking to determine whether they wish to make a life-transforming decision, may number several hundred. They are not excluded from participation in the family of faith, but it is clear that they have not yet chosen to step into the covenantal commitment.

5. Speak the truth in love. Daytop makes a great deal of the necessity of personal honesty and as much transparency as one can attain. I have a feeling that in terms of judgment,

this clue from Ephesians points a finger in several different directions. Sometimes clergy and congregations seek very hard to be loving fellowships and speak a great deal about the level of love that has been achieved. Often this smacks of very human levels of comaraderie rather than of significant *agape*, which can only come as a gift of God's grace. To feel at home and comfortable may be a sign of human homogeneity rather than the remarkable experience of the unity in diversity which Christ gives us. Also I am suspicious when someone announces that he or she loves everyone. So often the church uses the word "love" as though it were syrup poured over pancakes; whereas, clearly, love is a relationship that must have specificity to be genuine and does not occur simply because I will it. In a community of faith, I do not speak the truth in love unless the other person perceives that I am speaking in love. Therefore, I cannot control this relationship, but it is something that must be discovered in our life together. Life in community will only gradually take on the reality of truth in love as both I and the other discover that we do care for one another in Christ. Then we dare to risk of speaking the truth which is possible only in that unique context.

At times, congregations are very much given to speaking the truth, but with very little love. How easy it is to become harsh and judgmental in a way that is not a reflection of genuine concern for the other person, but simply one of affirming our own righteousness and indignation over the unfaithfulness or irresponsibility of other persons. "To speak the truth in love": this clearly is a critical clue for a nurturing community of faith. This goal is attainable only as our relationships with others have a degree of intimacy and intensity which will allow love to grow and the risk of speaking the truth to be undertaken.

I worked for several years as the assistant to an unusually

---

able woman pastor at one of the churches in the East Harlem. Protestant Parish. When she began her ministry, Letty Russell demanded in a variety of ways that in session meetings we speak the truth with as much love as we could muster. For a group of church officers, unaccustomed to open conflict and the expression of anger or vigorous disagreement, it was a very trying experience. But the after-session caucuses on the corner, the anger expressed in private were brought out into the open and a new level of trust and confidence enabled us to deal with issues of very heavy conflict and strong disagreement. Suddenly it became a reality to speak the truth in love. This is both a hard challenge and a glorious gift.

6. The pain of growth. In Ephesians, we are encouraged to be "no longer children, tossed to and fro and carried about with every wind of doctrine." It is hard to get used to the idea that when one does make a clear, mature, adult commitment to Jesus Christ as Lord we are in faith only one day old. As new members of God's household we then must pass through not only the years of childhood, adolescence, and young adulthood but for the rest of our lives must seek to grow toward Christian maturity in Christ. We will continually require a nurturing community. And nurture always comes at a cost. Can you remember any situation in your own life where there has been significant growth, new learning, and the achievement of new confidence that has not come at the cost of hard work, serious discipline and a certain amount of pain and frustration? To be part of the Daytop community demands a willingness to undergo very drastic surgery in terms of one's own life patterns. Perhaps nothing so overwhelming as this is necessary for many people in the household of faith, but certainly there need be no illusion about the necessity for discipline and hard work if we are to grow to

mature personhood, "to the measure of the stature of the fulness of Christ."

Yet a quick look at the average congregation indicates that what we undertake in the way of nurture is almost entirely directed toward Sunday school for children, with only a few adults participating in anything that would be considered a concrete educational enterprise and rarely any opportunity for continued nurture and growth. Adults have become Christian alumni; that is, they have graduated from the educational venture and are now concerned only to contribute to the alumni fund, to complain about the football coach, and to discuss how the present student generation does not measure up. But obedience allows no place for alumni.

B. *The Hope in Ephesians 4.* I long for the time when we will not push Ephesians 4 aside as irrelevant and impossible but will find in it also encouragement and hope. Here are clues that suggest how we might begin with our present congregations to move in the direction of fulfilling the nurturing function to lead the members to a far deeper identity in Christ. Let me suggest what some of these might look like. First is the question of *size*. Some years ago an Anglican priest named Ernest Southcott in Leeds, England, realized that when his congregation gathered primarily for worship on Sunday, there was little occasion for authentic community to develop. He began to experiment with the pattern of house churches. Members of the congregation were expected to gather at some point in the week in one another's homes for a service of Communion. Southcott found himself holding Mass before the members went off to work in the morning, using freshly baked bread in this familiar family setting of the dining room table. Morning, noon, and night, the big parish gathered in little families of faith, meeting through the parish area. A new sense of reality in the Christian life began to emerge.

The experience of Leeds makes clear the necessity of a nurturing community whose size makes possible family relationships which are given very concrete expression. The actual numbers may vary from extended families to small family units, but the important fact is that there is the possibility of mutually responsible, open, and continual relationships and a context for love and care.

A second element is that of *discipline*. A highly visible expression of this in Christian history comes in the Wesleyan class meeting. When John Wesley set out to find a new way of witnessing to the gospel in the emerging industrial society of eighteenth-century England, he quickly recognized that the experience of conversion which resulted from his preaching would have no lasting significance unless the men and women were quickly gathered into small communities of ten to fifteen members, "the class meeting" in which they would work at the question of the new habits of the Christian life and undertake the discipline which would enable them to be nurtured in their Christian maturity. The class meeting was really the secret of the explosive power of Methodism, whose impact on British history has been far in excess of the number of its members.

Another key word is *commitment*, or in biblical terms, the word *covenant*. When I listen to a clergyperson announce a prayer meeting on Wednesday night and say, "I urge everyone to come," I shudder. This laissez-faire optional nature of the Christian community is simply intolerable. It is far more effective to ask those who are prepared to undergo the discipline of a Bible study group to covenant with one another in terms of what they are prepared to do in the way of preparation, attendance, and duration. This is a way of establishing mutual responsibility and interdependence. Thus when one is absent, it is not just that person's loss, but the loss of the whole community. One, therefore, has a sense of responsibility toward the group as well as to one's self.

I am well aware that during the 60s, and even more recently, many congregations have experimented with "koinonia" groups, study groups, and a whole host of small group patterns through which they have sought to establish precisely what I am talking about in light of Ephesians 4. Success has not always resulted from the small group emphasis. I have struggled hard to recognize what has gone wrong. Why has this process not led to an authentic community of nurture after a strong spurt of enthusiasm has fizzled out? Several obvious reasons quickly become apparent. You cannot require or expect the present members of our congregations suddenly to become serious about the consequences of their faith. When men and women have been longtime members of the Christian community, there is no reason why they suddenly should be convinced that their involvement for the previous period was a mistake, or thoroughly inadequate, or not authentically Christian and then to undertake a new pattern. So many clergy, reading Southcott's book or other books in new life in the church, have informed their members that everyone has got to be part of a small study group in which they will fall in love with each other, learn to speak the truth, and express the variety of gifts. It simply is not a structure through which conversion usually takes place. The small community of faith is a place for those who have decided to be serious about their commitments and are willing to covenant together to create this new basis of community. Another obvious reason may be apparent in the very name, "koinonia" group. True community, genuine love for one another, is a gift to which we can be open but which dare not be the direct goal of our meeting. If we meet to deepen our faith or to learn to love one another, we almost certainly will be defeated by God. We have started at a point of self-centeredness. The small households of faith need desperately an objective purpose around which to gather, but one which provides the context in which the gift of love and growth can occur. One obvious objective purpose might simply be to overcome biblical illiteracy. A group may covenant to meet as a household of faith for six months to work on serious biblical study. Another group might meet around a missionary task or a functional need in the maintenance life of the congregation. When there is clearly defined work to be done that demands energy, discipline, faithfulness, and commitment, then we provide the context through which the Holy Spirit can be at work. No one dares comes with a blueprint for the successful community of faith. The question must always be, "How can we be open to the Spirit in this particular situation?" My own hunch is that whatever structures are created ought to be a function of a very clear mission task; whether it be a matter of service in the community or of an educational task in the life of the church or of maintenance, it is this context around which we may dare hope for the discovery of koinonia.

The problem, as expressed so often, is that of a large congregation some of whose members are serious about the faith and eager to grow in their own maturity, but many others of whose members are simply passengers on the boat, spectators, not serious participants in the Christian life. How can one proceed in this context without a sense of judgment on the passengers? It is realism to recognize that many of the members of our congregations have not yet discovered the freedom of the Christian life. They are still at the point of having their own needs met, rather than of being free to bear the burdens of others.

One parable illustrates an approach to this situation. Some years back, a young Methodist, a graduate of Union Theological Seminary, was called to be the student pastor for the Methodist men and women at a large southern university. He discovered on his arrival on the campus that there was a beautiful new Methodist student center halfway between the men's and women's campuses where he was expected to develop a fine Methodist student program. The Board of Higher Education in Nashville had given him a large book of directions on how to have a lively, vigorous activity program for Methodist students which would protect them from the evils of a large university. The present program was largely attended by freshmen and some sophomores. Juniors and seniors were hardly to be seen.

What kind of program would be possible? His decision was simplicity itself. He would seek ten sophomores and ten juniors who would commit themselves to a covenantal community that would meet for six to ten hours a week in study, worship, and life together. In this context he hoped they might discover the reality of Ephesians 4 and Acts 2:42. He would give these groups about half his time; but with the rest of his energy he would continue to maintain the program of the center, meeting the expectations of those who already were participating and of his ecclesiastic authorities. The vitality of the small groups was one of great dynamism and excitement. His ministry here was vital and satisfying. On the other hand, he discovered that his energy given to the original program was more effective than if he had been doing it full-time, but he was frustrated about that program's integrity. More important, he discovered that by the end of the first year many people out of the large activities program, with its traditional orientation, were intrigued by the covenantal community, excited by what was happening in the lives of those involved, and eager themselves to participate. Once again, demonstration of the power of the Spirit preceded explanation or proclamation. People in the larger program caught something of the reality of those who were taking seriously the consequences of their faith and deciding to make a covenantal commitment themselves. In some sense, is not this a parable for many of our congregations, a way by which we can provide centers around which those eager to grow in faith may gather while continuing as best we can and as faithfully as we know how to met the expectations of those who have gathered under the old ground rules?

A usual question at this point is this: "How does one avoid self-righteousness among those who are participating in the covenantal groups, the small households of faith?" The only answer I know is that if men and women are growing in maturity, if they are discovering the meaning of the Holy Spirit, then this leads to the gift of the Spirit— patience and forebearance, not judgment. Those who are discovering the freedom of Christ are ever more sensitive to their brothers and sisters in the larger community. Rather than being led to Pharisaism or self-righteousness, they grow more sensitive to their own continuing self-centered-ness and discover new freedom in caring for their brothers and sisters. The development of moral fiber frees us from the need to be judgmental. Where one finds men and women becoming exclusive, self-righteous over against those not serious about their faith, one can be sure that the Holy Spirit is not at work. They are not in a process of Christian nurture and growth.

In concluding this chapter, note that to be a nurturing community is perhaps the fundamental task of mission for the congregations of our day. Men and women have enlisted in a community whose purpose is to lead them to discover the freedom of the Christian life. To be a community of nurture may be the primary mission task on which our residential congregations, excluded from the world of significant public involvement, ought to focus. This is one imperative function of any community of faith. We do need structures of community other than the residential congregational base by which to engage in meeting the various missionary demands of Christ. A congregation which is not seriously nurturing its members is failing in a fundamental mission responsibility. A congregation, some of whose members are growing in maturity and faith, one whose members express the reality of a new kind of relationship in which Ephesians 4 comes alive, is in a powerful sense a political witness, a description in the midst of history of a sign of the kingdom of God that stands in judgment over against the values and social structures of our secular world. Where men and women break through the old sexist patterns, where racism no longer holds sway, where there is an expression of oneness in the lordship of Christ, there is a powerful judgment on the brokenness of our human communities and a sign, clearly written in history, of what God intends for all persons.

life in exile: a nurturing community

. . . "My son, do not regard lightly the discipline of the Lord, nor lose courage when you are punished by him.

"For the Lord disciplines him whom he loves, and chastises every son whom he receives." —Hebrews 12:5-6. Read Hebrews 12:5-13.

The Meaning of "Truly Human"

In our consideration of Ephesians 4 in the last chapter, I skirted a full consideration of verse 13. What does the author mean in talking about mature personhood, "the measure of the stature of the fulness of Christ"? What kind of specificity can the Christian bring in talking about the meaning of new life in Christ? Some years ago, Professor Paul Lehmann wrote an excellent book on Christian ethics with the theme "the task of the church is to make and keep human life truly human." He was, of course, using Aristotle's definition, which described the work of the politican as the art of making and keeping human life truly human. I found this phrase, as a way of describing the life and work of the church, very exciting and helpful but lacking in specifics. A truly human life is experienced when one is clear and consistent about both one's identity and one's vocation. Identity is a way of saying in shorthand that human beings are given the unique capacity of self-transcendence. We are able to stand outside ourselves, examining our past and our future as the base for making decisions in the present. Someone has called this the ability to see ourselves in the mirror. We are historical animals who experience the past with its meaning in order to make decisions that guide us into the future. Perhaps our forebearers first became truly human when they began to bury their ancestors, developing in this way a symbolic sense of their own history. Another way to talk about identity is to speak about our capacity to worship. In making the important decisions of life, every one of us inevitably must have criteria by which we can make decisions, about both minor and major matters. Insofar as we are simply determined by habits instilled in us or by instincts we express nothing uniquely human. But insofar as we exercise our capacity for self-transcendence and make choices based on some conscious criteria we are expressing our humanity. Years ago Robert Calhoun talked about a man's religion being defined by the object of his ultimate loyalty and devotion; that is, the criteria, the meaning, the goals which we apply to our conscious living.

Using Calhoun's criteria, I suppose most of us are pantheists; in different areas of our lives and activities we demonstrate loyalty to quite different goals and values rather than to one clear and explicit commitment. But to say it again, insofar as we are aware of the criteria for our decisions and conscious about our own identity as actors in our own history, to that degree we express our full humanity.

The other word which I would emphasize is "vocation." We are political animals in the sense that men and women must participate in building community. Animals live in herds. People live in society and are responsible for creating their own institutions, economics, politics, family, and the rest. Only as we express this God-given capacity for community building, take responsibility for shaping the world of which we are a part, to that degree we express authentic humanity. When we are allowed to express this capacity, then to that degree we become a person. In his fascinating book, *Pedagogy of the Oppressed*, Paolo Freire describes in very vivid terms the way in which peasants in Brazil recovered a sense of humanity when they came to understand the forces that operated on them in their own society were created not by fate but by realities which could be named and understood. Relieved of a sense of personal guilt or fatalism, they were able then to become actors in their own history even though they still faced serious problems of oppression. It was this understanding of their ability to name the forces of oppression and to function as responsible people within them that restored in them the image of God.

When persons are denied identity or denied the opportunity of expressing their vocation in caring for and building community, to that degree dehumanization is inevitable. In a nutshell, that is the tragedy of slavery in the United States and its continuing expression in racism. For black men and women to be taught in myriad ways that black was evil and to be cut off from their African history, and denied that possibility for identity was totally dehumanizing. The problem, of course, was not resolved by the end of official slavery. During the height of the civil rights movement, I remember a beautiful black woman trying to get across the anguish which comes when black persons are denied the right to affirm their identity. She said that as a small child her mother used to say, "Thelma, you're as good as any little white child. Thelma, don't ever forget you're as good as any little white child," as she spent an hour trying to straighten her child's naturally kinky hair. In a myriad of ways, we have done this to those who are not of white skin.

At the same time, the Negro in American History, in affirming the beauty of blackness and recovering something of the power of identity, has still faced the difficulty in expressing the human capacity and necessity for political involvement. In slavery the opportunity for participation in responsible decision-making was completely denied. But since the Civil War, the difficulty the black faced in participating in politics, at least until very recently and even now significantly, and the limitations on economic opportunity have been a poignant source of oppression. Racism, in its most vicious sense, denies humanity to men and women when it limits their ability to affirm their own identity and to express their vocation through participation in shaping history.

Another pointed illustration of the limitation of humanity comes from Betty Friedan's remarkable book, written nearly fifteen years ago now, called *The Feminine Mystique*. The fact that this sold over a million copies in its early years of publication indicates that it was saying something of tremendous importance to the middle-class, largely white American women who read it in such great numbers. It was a book not about sex, but about the sexism of American life. Betty Friedan described in the book the life-style expected of women. American women had been taught that they need not bother their pretty little heads about anything to do with the areas of politics or the public sector. They were the most blessed women in human history. All they needed to do was to live in a lovely suburban home, be a chauffeur to their children, and be an attractive mistress to their husband; and life would be a ball. In a word, they were told not to worry about involvement in any of the responsibilities for the world of which they were a part other than in the personal, private, family sector. Ms. Friedan looked through countless women's magazines without discovering a single article which had to do with substantive discussion of world affairs, economics, politics, or any other such critical public sector problems. The feminine mystique was the strange feeling of emptiness and unfulfillment that women felt, about which they had a sense of guilt since they were supposed to be so blessed and happy. Betty Friedan put her finger on the profound dehumanization of the American woman and called forth the critical struggle for liberation which has been expressed by women's movements ever since.

Up to this point I have not in any way tried to express these realities of humanity in Christian terms, but the connection is simple. To be truly human for a Christian is to discover one's identity in loyalty to Christ and one's vocation in the servanthood to Christ. This is not necessarily a different expression of humanity as over against what is possible for other men and women. I recognize this as a debatable point. Has it not been a real mistake in much Christian theology to assume that only Christians are able to express full maturity, that it is possible only for those who consciously name the name of Christ? Knowing as Christians this experience of true humanity, do we not discover it expressed also in those who do not know the name of Christ but in their lives express his presence and concern? Christians, in identifying with the image of Christ, are simply affirming that to be truly human is to be free from self-love and focused in obedience and love for his world. In a community like East Harlem, one continually comes across men and women who have been given this selflessness and humility. They turn their attention to bearing the burdens of others rather than upon their own self-centered needs.

Meanwhile the churches of our day in so many situations express little of the reality of Christ. In order to obey Christ many of those who are led by the Spirit of God have had to reject the institution and think in the process they have rejected Christ. But God works through far more of us than those who are self-conscious about our faith and thus accept the name of Christ. I remember a challenging lecture by E. R. Wickham, at that time leader of the Industrial Mission Project in Sheffield, England. He told the students that he was always saddened when someone who was discovering the power of the gospel in the Industrial Mission program and seeking to make his faith effective in the work of the industrial complex in Sheffield decided he needed to become a participant in the local parish. He then had no time left for expressing his vocation but was absorbed in the introverted activities of the institution and removed from any significant obedience. Does this sometimes ring true for us?

We reserve the name of Christian, however, for those who consciously find their identity in Christ and let their lives be shaped by him. To live in him is to be free to love and care as he was free to love and care. God made a world in which he gave us responsibility for our own destiny, in which we are by nature political, so not only are we free to love and care, we also must live in community and take responsibility for it. The Christian seeks to express this political responsibility by following the pattern of the ministry of Jesus in service and witness.

In summary of what has been said here, let me offer a diagram.

WORSHIP = IDENTITY = THE STATURE OF CHRIST

POLITICS = VOCATION = SERVANTHOOD IN CHRIST

We have used previously the biblical expression "signs of shalom." In the New Testament, Paul also used the phrase "the first fruits of the kingdom." A congregation which is in no sense perfect but where men and women are seeking to grow in their identity in Christ and to express their vocation is a powerful sign of first fruits, a taste in the midst of human history now of what God's kingdom ultimately will be like. It is a sign, a guarantee of what is coming, of what is possible for all people. To test the integrity of a congregation, see if those who are participants are involved in the pain of growth, are able more and more frequently to express the love of Christ in their own personhood, and are wrestling with faithfulness in their participation in whatever "political" arena is appropriate. Identity is "looking to Jesus the pioneer and perfector of our faith" (Hebrews 12:2). Vocation is "If any man would come after me, let him deny himself and take up his cross daily and follow me" (Luke 9:23). These define full humanity for those who take the name of Christ.

A Critique of Nurture in the Congregation

The congregations that are typical of most of American church life are, of course, basically located in communities where men and women reside, where the energy and interests which are operative within the sphere of the church tend to be those that have most to do with identity and only partially with the expression of vocation. I think it only appropriate then that the congregation understand the great urgency of the task of nurture and accept the limitation of the areas of vocational involvement and public responsibility in which it must function. This is partly expressed in the argument in the period of the missionary structure debate. As Howard Moody said so specifically, "Even if we could renew as faithful communities of nurture and mission every residential parish in the United States, we would still need many new forms through which

Christians may appropriately involve themselves in the public sector and meet the needs for witness and service in an urban, technological society." But that leaves the residential parish with primary nurturing responsibility. Failure to fulfill effectively the primary nurturing function is a serious matter.

There is no stronger critique than the picture painted in *The Feminine Mystique.* The fact that the majority of clergy have never heard of the book, to say nothing of having read it, is a powerful judgment on the church. The women who read *The Feminine Mystique* are the members of our active and lively suburban congregations. We have not understood their pain.

If we have little significant nurture for adults at least we run Sunday schools. But little is healthy even here. For a good many years now I have worked with a group of thirty college students from a fine New England private college who spend a seven-week academic term working in East Harlem. I ask them at the beginning of our academic sessions to write out a definition of their own religious faith—that is, what is important to them in life—and then to describe any ways in which participation in religious institutions have had any effect on their life faiths. For eight years now, the experience of reading those papers has been absolutely consistent. Almost everyone of the students, whether man or woman, has been brought up in a religious community, primarily Protestant churches in the New England states: Methodist, Baptist, United Church of Christ for the most part. What the papers prove, beyond a shadow of a doubt is the massive failure of our Christian education programs. The amount of misinformation and ignorance which is expressed in those papers means that Sunday schools are not simply neutral—by neutral I mean they don't teach very much—they are also harmful. I state this strongly and with very great feeling. Perhaps the most obvious explanation is that children are not dumb. When Sunday schools are taught for less than an hour once a week with often inadequate teachers, the children get the point very quickly. Instead of the Christian faith's being a matter of central importance through which one understands all of life, it is simply an activity which you do with a little piece of your time in an often boring classroom on Sunday morning.

Before any reader gets upset with this strong language, I suggest that you look carefully and as objectively as possible at the Sunday school and youth program in your own church. What are its specific goals and what measures are you using to determine whether these are in any significant sense being achieved? How often do we keep our children in Sunday school only until they have enough independence to break out, usually just after being led through the normative communicant's or church membership class, somewhere between the ages of ten and fourteen. Those who continue in the youth program tend to be a very limited number who have nothing better to do. On occasion there are really "successful" youth programs which meet a profound social need for young people but may have only a limited relationship to the function of a community of faith. Just take a look at what is happening and pray that by the grace of God what I have said does not fit your particular situation.

Gabriel Moran is a Roman Catholic theologian, uniquely creative in contemporary church life. He wrote somewhere that he woke up one morning and asked himself the question, "Moran, whoever told you that Christian education was for children?" He went on to explain that for a good many years he had been trying to train teachers for the Catholic schools and to develop new curriculum in relationship to new theological understanding, but the whole effort never quite seemed to come off. He asked the iconoclastic question, "What is Christian education trying to do anyway?" and came to the very simple answer—Christian education is the nurturing task of the Christian community for men and women who after adolescence have made an adult commitment to Jesus Christ and want to engage in serious study that will enable them to grow to the maturity of Christ. This strikes me as being a very telling definition. We allow children to make no other life commitments until the maturity of young adulthood begins to emerge, but we force them into church membership classes or communicant's courses at the point in their lives when they are still under both the tremendous authority of parents and the pressure of the peer group. What kind of an answer is it to say, "If we don't get them now, it will be too late"? It is high time we began to trust in the Holy Spirit to lead men and women to faith without that kind of dehumanizing manipulation. I will in a moment talk about our educational responsibility to children and young people, but that is not our primary Christian educational task. Let us now take a look at clues for adult education and nurturing. A program for those who are serious about their growth in Christ is the heart of Christian education.

Clues for Adult Education

I have no argument with the fine adult education materials prepared by most denominations and see no need here either to critique or to support what is readily available for men and women who wish to involve themselves in the serious study of the commitment they have made and who look for objective tasks which will enable, by the grace of God, a community of faith to emerge. The challenge does not lie with educational materials but with a new understanding of the nature of nurture. I want to suggest a framework for thinking about this question and then make several footnotes to what is described in *The Congregation in Mission*.

The text I would suggest is in Hebrews 12. The first thirteen verses are well worth reading (as is the whole chapter). Here the emphasis is upon discipline, discipline as two elements: God's chastisement upon our failures and, more important, the discipline with which parents seek to help children to mature to authentic personhood. The latter is the discipline of the athlete who prepares for the contest. It is the discipline of the recruit in the military, who must be relieved of his civilian habits and responses in order to be prepared for the demands of the new life which has been accepted by enlistment. The Bible is, of course, full of such military metaphors, having often taken over from secular culture images and conceptions which were then used in the church. For example, the word "sacramentum" in Latin was the oath which a civilian took when he entered the legions of Caesar. So by the sacrament of baptism does the Christian enter into the discipline of the Christian community.

The word "discipline" is not a comfortable one for many Christian communities, though it relates simply to the question of becoming a disciple. D. T. Niles gave us the idea of replacing the word "discipline" with the word "habits" of the Christian life. I well remember my own experience of joining the United States Navy, where in boot camp we went through several months of hard drills and training, both often tiring and utterly boring but critical if I were to achieve a new style of life replacing my normal civilian habits. In a sense then, the congregation is a boot camp for Christians, that seeks to discipline us in the habits of life which open us to the continuing gifts and presence of the

Holy Spirit. Basic habits are defined, as suggested earlier, by those four elements in Acts 2:42. They include Bible study, prayer, fellowship, and communion. After boot camp comes special training school where I was taught to be a gunnery officer. Boot camp equipped me with the habits of the military, my identity, while gunnery school was for my particular "vocation." I needed a community of nurture in which I could be equipped for my particular vocation as a gunnery officer on a destroyer escort. It is these two motifs which sometimes require quite different schools or communities of nurture. This understanding may relieve the residential congregation from the impractical task of having to fulfill both functions. To use the military metaphor just one step further, the congregation can also be a base of rest and rehabilitation, a place to which one returns from pilgrimage for a new sense of understanding and identity.

In terms of the essential habits of the Christian life stressed in Acts 2:42, a few comments are in order.

A. *Biblical literacy is a critical element in the Christian life.* It simply makes no sense to say that Jesus Christ is Lord and not be as familiar as possible with the whole landscape of what God did in Israel, the history of the biblical faith, and certainly the New Testament, both the Jesus stories and the life of the early church. But it is obvious that biblical illiteracy is the norm in the church. Recently a group of us were teasing the new professor of homiletics at Union Theological Seminary, James Forbes, as to what sense it made for him to try to preach teaching at Union. He responded that he did indeed have a problem. In the black church from which he comes, The United Holiness Church of America, he said you can always take for granted two elements: "The congregation believes the Scriptures have authority and they really know the Scriptures." He indicated rather reluctantly that at Union Theological Seminary you could not assume either of these preparations in the students who entered his homiletics classroom. But that is precisely the point. If we are to look at the world with eyes of faith, the Scriptures must be familiar territory. One problem, I suggest, is to recapture the Bible from the scholars. The biblical guild has in effect made it quite obvious that only a biblical scholar through hard years of disciplined study can interpret the Scriptures accurately. This model is then made adequately clear to future clergy who struggle to be second-rate biblical scholars, interpreting the Scriptures to their laity. Thank God the whole history of the church indicates that when men and women have direct access to the words of faith, they can hear and understand with power and authenticity.

Professor Walter Wink in his little book *The Bible in Human Transformation* and in other writings has been a great help in underlining the need for the recovery of the Scriptures by ordinary Christian men and women. Professor Thomas Boomershine, equally in anguish over the problem of scholarly ownership of the Scriptures, has been developing a fascinating method of storytelling as a way of opening with excitement the Scriptures to laity. His argument is very simple. By taking the Scriptures apart, biblical scholars overlook the fact that, however they arrived at their final version, the Scriptures come to us as a whole cloth and are certainly meant to be told and heard, not read and pulled apart. Boomershine has helped men and women learn to memorize the stories in a way which makes them available with fresh and dramatic excitement. Studying the Bible becomes a far more vital experience than simply reading the Scriptures or listening to someone explain them. In our experience in East Harlem men and women, often with little literary background or even developed reading skills, could, in hearing the stories of the Bible, react to them with excitement and understanding.

B. *In Acts 2:42, the second emphasis is upon* prayer. Again, there are far too many good books on the topic (for example: George A. Buttrick, *Prayer;* John B. Coburn, *Prayer and Personal Religion;* Mark Gibbard, *Why Pray?;* and John R. Yungblut, *Rediscovering Prayer*) for me to try to add anything original except for one footnote. Prayer is seeking time and time again, alone and corporately, to reflect on our lives in the light of what God is doing in Jesus Christ. It is not so much a matter of petition, the focus of so much we call prayer, as it is a matter of seeking to be open, to see with eyes of faith, to understand, to be judged, and then to act again. Bonhoeffer in *Life Together* has written the classic in the corporate nature of prayer. I have reread it many times.

For me the meaning of individual prayer most helpful has been in the experience of the Iona Community. Dr. George Macleod, the founder, introduced me to the "ordered day." First he described arising in the morning with thanks to God for the night's sleep and the new day. Then he would "pray through" the events that clearly were scheduled for the day, seeking to reflect upon what might be demanded in the light of his Christian commitment and thus prepare himself for the challenges both expected and unexpected that might emerge. Then during the course of the day, prayer was the continually seeking to be open to the assurance that his life was to be a sign of God's presence, that he was not his own, but Christ's. He said this often meant that, in a tense session, suddenly he would be reminded not to fight for his own ego or needs, but to look again at what it was that God was seeking to express in that situation. That didn't mean any easy answer, but it did mean a sensitivity beyond his own needs and a new perspective. Then as the day closed, he would reflect again on the events of the day, praying, laying before God those whose needs he had encountered, asking forgiveness for the places where he failed, and then offering up to God the work of that day and again his own life. Something like this is what I take to be the life of prayer as a personal discipline.

C. *The Christian community in Acts 2:42 was involved in* communion; *that is, the life of corporate worship.* Worship for the Christian community is sometimes spoken of as if it were an end in itself, as though what happens in church on Sunday morning is the be all and end all of the Christian community. To be present for the mass, for the liturgy, or for the service of preaching is what determines the degree of one's commitment. I find this increasingly intolerable. When the community gathers it is part of a much larger rhythm of its life. God has placed us in the world for witness and service. When we gather at his table, it is to reflect on what we have been doing, to seek insight for what we will do, and to offer up our lives as a community before God. But the integrity of our lives around that table or before the pulpit depends very much upon what we have done before and what we will do afterward in our obedience.

Insofar as the gathering of the congregation for worship reflects the disunity of the church in its class and racial nature we may also need to be very nervous. If the church gathered is not a sign of shalom, does not express the first fruits of the kingdom, then I somehow think we may be vulnerable to Paul's challenge in First Corinthians 11: "Whoever, therefore, eats the bread or drinks the cup of the Lord in an unworthy manner will be guilty of profaning the body and blood of the Lord." Is he perhaps talking about a congregation which expresses a homogeneity of race or class that by its very gathering points away from our new unity in Christ?

D. *Finally in Acts 2:42 the gathering of the Christian community was for the sake of* fellowship. In our life together we must be about the task of discovering our gifts of the Spirit and seeking to discipline them for the sake of their effectiveness. When I discern in myself or in others gifts of the Spirit which are necessary for building up the body of Christ, those gifts still must be given support, encouragement, and, I suspect, a good deal of nurturing for the sake of their proper usefulness. When I as a pastor discover in the congregation a woman blessed with compassion and sensitivity to the needs of others, it is my job to give her confidence in those gifts and the technical knowledge which will enable her to use them with greatest effectiveness in the service of others.

Under this heading of fellowship I am also concerned about every gathering of the congregation, whether for a committee meeting, a session of the governing board of trustees, or a social event. Is it not our task to make sure that every gathering for whatever mundane purpose is seen not as a business operation or an administrative session but as an occasion for deepening our relations with each other and for growth in our understanding of the nature and the purpose of the church? How easy it is to let maintenance tasks be isolated from our nurturing responsibilities in a way that quickly becomes dysfunctional.

The Nurture of Children

The Christian education enterprise has been subject to plenty of criticism in our day in spite of the valiant efforts of denominational staffs to provide us with excellent education materials. As Gabriel Moran suggests, it seems to me that the problem is not with the level of materials for Sunday school classes or youth programs, but in the very nature and context in which we engage in the task. I suggest that we should not call our responsibility for children "Christian education." Then we make one dehumanizing assumption; namely, that when we baptize our children or dedicate them at a tender age, we have already made the decision that they are to be Christians whether they like it or not. Jewish boys are circumcised. You are born a Jew, and for the rest of your life, you can be either a good Jew or a bad Jew, but you can't be a non-Jew. In contrast, the Christian community has always affirmed the necessity of a personal decision to make Jesus Christ one's Lord. To assume that this happens prior to the end of adolescence is in most cases, I affirm, close to blasphemy. We do not trust the Holy Spirit. What we are about with children and with young people is to provide a context in which the hope expressed in baptism and our commitment made then can have a chance to blossom in the family of faith. But we must never force them to assume, no matter how subtly, that the decision has been made so they have no choice but to be a good Christian or a bad Christian. In spite of sound theological doctrine to the contrary, the ethos of the Christian community does force this assumption down the throats of our children almost universally.

What is appropriate education for our children in the church? It is that the child's experience in the community of faith be one of love, acceptance, and affirmation. The community of God's people is a family in which children should be loved, disciplined, and affirmed as in a human family. Part of the urgency of my concern lies in the fact that so many children in our day, in the broken homes of suburbia as well as in the inner city, will find the experience of a nurturing community only in the church rather than in their own homes. In East Harlem, we could not use the experience of the children in their own families as metaphors for the relationships in the kingdom of God. But the biblical pattern is no different. When Jesus teaches us about God as father, he enables a human father to know what his role is to be. The relationship between Jesus and his disciples is an illustration of the life appropriate to a Christian community. To make the point again, we do well to avoid calling this important ministry with children "Christian" education. We do have a critical nurturing task, but it involves far more than the lessons in a classroom for an hour once a week. Here we are not talking about simply teaching the content of the Christian faith or pouring a certain amount of biblical facts into the heads of our children. The Christian commitment at its best provides an environment that enables the child to grow in the experiences which open young human lives to discovering the authenticity of the Christian faith. It is important then that the community offer at least the following:

1. *A place where the child is affirmed as a person.* In a sense, the Christian is always a nonconformist. There is no one type of personhood required, only the affirmation of the uniqueness of each one of us that allows for the child to become the one whom God intends. Perhaps this is only to say the Christian community must be a place where children are truly loved and affirmed for who they are.

2. *A place where ancestor stories are told.* I have been impressed with the excitement children find in the biblical stories of both the Old and the New Testament when they are told for what they are: the stories of their own ancestors. I am a child of Abraham, Isaac, and Jacob, of Moses and

Isaiah and Jeremiah. The story of the New Testament is my story. I want to tell them to children with the same excitement with which my father told me about his life on a farm in Eddyville, Iowa, where he grew up on the frontier. The stories of faith are exciting and beautiful when told without some need to force a moral down in the end. A discovery of our heritage is important to human growth; but when the stories are told by teachers who do not find them significant in their own heritage, or who little understand them, or who feel the need to use them as ethical lessons, the whole game falls to pieces and we quickly find our children bored. In fact, there are all kinds of ways to act out or make the stories of faith come alive.

3. *A place where children are free to question and to challenge.* In our educational processes in secular society we almost always train children to believe that everything has a right and a wrong answer. We also fall into the trap in Sunday school of acting as though for every question we have a clear answer. The Bible is full of men and women who question and challenge and cry out against the crises of life, often getting no better answers than Job got. As a growing person the child has every right to ask questions without the adult's always assuming that he has got to come back with an answer. The important thing is to stir the imaginations of children rather than to bottle them up by putting a cork, called "answer," in every question. But what a challenge this is to teachers to have the personal self-confidence to allow the imagination of children to grow and expand.

4. *Freedom to opt out.* Erik Erikson, in discussing his seven stages of life, talks about the need for a psychosexual moratorium. Young people in our culture are prepared for adulthood in home, church, and school. The programming

they receive is often very clear about how to act, what to believe, and what to become. Even the child of poverty is drenched by the media with a very clear image of the "good life." Erikson suggests that we do not establish adult maturity until we have a chance to step back from these socializing structures and discover our own commitments and values. Children who are found in the youth program of a church are often those who have not questioned rigorously the values of their parents, their school, or their church in order to achieve their own identity. But maturity demands that we discover for ourselves out of our heritage what is valuable and critical for us. Without the opportunity for appropriate questioning or even rebelling, children often break free in adolescence or young adulthood in a far more terrifying way than when freedom to question, to challenge, to rethink, and to opt out is allowed graciously. In recent years I have spent much time trying to convince parents that when their teen-age son or daughter decides to drop out of college for a year or two it may be the most creative and helpful thing that could possibly happen. To fight it, however, is to look for trouble.

One quick illustration of the problem of our young people: So many of those who decide on the ordained Christian ministry have not been through a moratorium but have decided on this vocation as a teen-ager at a youth conference. They continued in the church as a youth leader and went on to a denominational college where they were part of the preministerial group and then went to theological seminary. How often these graduates of a theological seminary wake up at the age of thirty or thirty-five asking, "How in heaven's name did I get here? Do I really affirm this Christian faith as my own? Did I really want to be a minister or did I get programmed into this by the tunnels of family, church, and school at a far too tender age?" It could revolutionize theological education at one fell swoop, if no student were allowed to enter seminary who had not been involved for at least several years in intense living outside of the protection of academia, church, and family in order to discover his or her own identity.

vocation of pilgrims: seek the shalom of the city

Read Luke 4:16-21.

The Challenge of Jeremiah

Exile came to the Hebrew people as a shock. Jeremiah turned it into a challenge. Even in Babylon they could live with meaning, still affirm their identity as God's people, continue the rhythms of life. But then came an even more baffling bit of advice. They were to find the purpose of their lives, the expression of their God-given vocation, in seeking the welfare of Babylon: "Seek the welfare of the city where I have sent you into exile, and pray to the Lord on its behalf, for in its welfare you will find your welfare." One can imagine the advice they might have expected. They would have been prepared for his suggesting one of the usual options for those in exile. An obvious choice might have been seeking to escape, to figure out ways by which they might in some numbers elude their captors and return to their homeland. Exiles have the choice of rebellion, or at least subversion. They can make life miserable for their captors by throwing monkey wrenches in the machinery of the community and finding subtle and secret ways to mess up the society of which they are a part. Occasionally, this option can take the form of armed rebellion; but, in any case, there are a variety of ways in which they can express their hostility and anger. A third, perhaps more customary, option in the face of the military might of the oppressor is simply to survive, whether it be by existing in apathy or turning completely inward to one's own survival needs. The result is always dehumanizing, for to live simply day by day with no sense of a future is to warp one's personhood.

The parallel to these three options in the inner city like East Harlem is all too poignant. The heavy incidence of drug addiction is simply the most vicious form of readily available escape. By every turn of the television dial and by the media in general, the young person is told that in America he is in the land of opportunity, but then discovers at the age of thirteen or fourteen that the future really doesn't exist if you are black or poor in the United States (statistically speaking). Then, the only apparent way to make your dreams come true is by the opiate of narcotics.

A more acceptable form of escape can also come through religion which becomes a survival technique for so many, a place to escape the pain of tenement living and dehumanized employment or the more dehumanizing welfare system, a place to find some personal identity or meaning night after night in a small community of faith.

The option of rebellion is equally obvious. The events in New York City in July, 1977, when the city for twenty-four hours had a "whiteout," are one dramatic evidence that no commitment to our society has been inculcated into thousands of urban dwellers whose alienation took the form of spontaneous looting on that long, hot night. Rebellion is expressed in the senseless violence toward the elderly, in the gangs and crimes so endemic in our cities. We all pay a terrible price when a sector of our society lives in dehumanized exile from the opportunities and values of the main culture.

In the inner city there is also survival, the kind best described by the word "apathy." This is to live day by day without a sense of past or future that leads one toward authentic personhood. I shall never forget reading a study of chronic truants in an East Harlem junior high school. When I was a youngster and someone played hooky, it was because there was a better thing to do—the circus had come to town or it was time to go fishing. But the researchers, in looking at the lives of twenty chronic truants, discovered that these young boys were found at home sitting in a room and listening to the radio or watching TV, simply existing. In a poignant question, the delinquents were asked "What do you want to be when you grow up?" The response uniformly was to draw a blank. These students had, as the report said, "no hopes, no dreams, no visions for the future." At the age of twelve or thirteen, life simply had closed in. Without a past with memories upon which to build or a future toward which to work and hope, they simply existed, not much different than a pet animal. This is apathy in its most painful expression.

These usual options of escape, rebellion, or survival are all ignored by Jeremiah in his advice. His word is to seek the welfare of that community where we have been placed by God as his witnesses. Unfortunately, the churches of our time, certainly in the mainline denominations, have usually chosen a fourth option rather than accept Jeremiah's advice. To put it bluntly, the white middle-class church has joined the enemy and decided that its welfare lies in solidarity with the culture of which it is a part. I write this less as an accusation than as a hypothesis which needs to be tested in every situation where the church finds itself successfully and comfortably at home, most obviously in a suburban environment. Kilmer Myers in a beautiful little book about his early ministry, *Light the Dark Streets,* wrote that a congregation not in tension with its environment could not be a church of Jesus Christ. Where is the tension and challenge between your congregation and its community? Another way to look at it is through an interesting quotation from Peter Berger. He wrote in a *Christianity and Crisis* article, "in America we have a secularized church in a pseudo-Christian culture." Where that is the case, there is no significant dialogue, encounter, or confrontation between the church and the world. Churches simply live in peaceful harmony without creative tension. This quotation from Berger is from an article in which he seeks to compare the evangelical academies in Europe after World War II with the American situation. In Western Europe, where Christianity had become such a minority factor, there was an important role for dialogue and confrontation between the insights of the Christian community and that of the secular world. These encounters were made possible by a group of dialogue centers called evangelical academies. Berger's conclusion was that the evangelical academies were impossible in the United States since a kind of syncretism existed which made dialogue irrelevant.

For a congregation in a middle-class white suburb, syncretism is a very grim problem. The suburb closest to New York City is named Bronxville. Until recently, not even a Jew was allowed to buy a house in Bronxville despite the law, to say nothing of a black family. You had to be a white Christian to live there. When the workers in the local hospital—maintenance and cleaning personnel, orderlies, and the like—sought without success to gain recognition for their union and went on strike, they found a hostile community uniformly against them. These workers, unable to live in Bronxville, commuted out from Harlem and other parts of New York City for their jobs in the local hospital. When several members of a local congregation sought to learn the workers' side of the story, they discovered that many of the employees of the hospital in wealthy Bronxville earned so little under the minimum wage that they required welfare supplements in New York City. They felt there was something to be said in behalf of the workers. A letter to the local newspaper suggesting that perhaps there were two sides to the story brought immediate vilification from the other members of the community. They were treated like pariahs in their local congregation and their own doctors told them that they would never treat them again. I mention this little vignette only to make clear why many of us have sought ministry in the inner city, where the identification of the church with the needs of the exile community made it far easier to define the enemy and stand over against the pressures which denied the values of our faith than it ever is for a pastor in a suburban community. To be a Christian and an exile in the inner city is certainly culturally and sociologically far more easy an option than to seek in a suburban context to uphold an exile posture in the face of the uniform hostility of the whole community. To say it again, I am not trying to be cynical about the problems of a suburban congregation in identifying so closely with its culture. Rather, I am hoping that, in reflecting on Jeremiah's advice, our "successful" congregations might look again at the possibility of fulfilling an exile mandate even in the midst of their present acceptance.

This can only happen when the churches do not meet simply one among many needs of the suburban dweller or middle-class Christian but become the center from which all of life takes on its meaning and direction. You can neither be a part-time exile or pilgrim, nor can you limit your area of commitment to a certain sector of life. This is the issue raised by James Cone in *Black Theology and Black Power*. In that book, half a dozen times he asked the question rather poignantly, "Could you white middle-class Christians tell me how you can say that for you Jesus Christ is Lord and not in some significant way identify with the black and the poor and the oppressed in our country?' Cone is expressing the problem of privatized religion. Very dedicated and committed men and women have seen their personal lives transformed by a new relationship with Jesus Christ. It has profoundly changed their personal relationships with family and friends, but there is an almost complete absence of any commitment to public problems and social ills. It has changed their relationships, but has not given them a new set of relationships. It has not made them sensitive to the anguish of the poor in their own communities or the problems of the war in Vietnam. They have not been led, in Cone's words, to any kind of "new participation with the problems of the black and the poor and the oppressed." They have not discovered that Christ has given them new neighbors. Unless our commitment to Jesus is expressed in a new capacity for seeking the welfare of the community where we have been placed, we have identity without vocation and our faith will soon become atrophied or heretical.

The Caring Task

In this chapter, I am concerned about the church as a caring community dealing with issues that are normally called social welfare, a community that deals with problems crying out for healing and compassion. Later we shall look at the requirements for prophetic action and public involvement with the principalities and powers. Together they are the crucial elements that go into seeking the welfare of the city. Note that the word in Hebrew is "shalom." Seek the shalom of the city; that is, its peace and justice, its fulfillment of joy and meaning for God's children and all his creation.

I suspect that there is no congregation that does not accept and recognize a very fundamental concern to be a loving and caring community for those who participate in its life. We are participants because the church is our family, in which we find support and love when we face the crises and unexpected challenges of our lives. I want in no way to denigrate or criticize the importance of the church as this kind of caring community. But I do want to suggest that this is precisely the nature of a variety of human communities, beginning with our own families, and to argue very strenuously that the church's commitment to care for its own must be transmuted into caring for those outside its gathered life. Our concern is not for the exile community, but for Babylon. Strange as this advice may be, clearly this is God's word to us.

A New Testament text that stands out in this regard comes in the very beginning of the ministry of Jesus. You will recall that after the temptation in the wilderness, Jesus returned to Nazareth and, as his custom was, attended the synagogue on the Sabbath. There he was offered the chance to read from the Scriptures, and he read the powerful passage from Isaiah 61. As reported in Luke 4:16-21, Jesus in effect defines the nature of his own ministry in quite specific terms. It is to preach good news to the poor, to release the captives, help the blind recover their sight, and to set at liberty those who are oppressed. Beginning from that point forward, Jesus' own life is clearly defined by his profound caring for those who are infirm in body, mind, or spirit. Whether it was a paralytic man, whose need was both to be forgiven of his sins and healed of his infirmity, or a man born blind, or a woman with an issue of blood, Jesus' own life expressed his compassion and his healing commitment. These were powerful signs of the Kingdom.

So it must be with his church. Our inevitable concentric concern for our own people and our own needs cries out to be transformed into an ex-centric commitment, a concern for those whose needs around us are obvious and urgent. Yet how easy it is for us to delude ourselves into thinking we are caring for others when we maintain our basic institutional self-centeredness. We simply are not there in a way that seeks the welfare of the city. Yet the times cry out for Christian presence and concern.

As congregations look at the task of caring, let me suggest a list of criteria, factors in style, which may be helpful clues in determining what we must be about and how we must be about doing it. This is simply a checklist for our task of caring.

A. *Participation.* This factor is in contrast to a very pervasive style of paternalism. Paternalism means that those who do the caring do so in a manner that treats the recipients of their care as children or incompetents. Christian benevolence often has a way of helping the less fortunate, of seeking to share our largesse with those who stand in great need, while keeping ourselves safely over and above them. In the movie "Monsieur Vincent," there is a telling scene where a group of wealthy society women come to see the urban priest whom they have been assisting once a month as volunteers. The wealthy Parisian women were very upset because, as they said, they had been coming there for some months now and the poor people didn't seem grateful. Monsieur Vincent, the sensitive Catholic priest, says quite simply, "My dears, when you give your alms to the poor, be grateful that they do not hate you."

Paternalism is also reflected in a familiar phrase in the social work jargon, "servicing our clients," as though the people who use the welfare agencies of our city are to be treated somewhat like an automobile at a gas station. Participation is rather a reflection of a sincere involvement of those who are helpers in the lives of those to whom we direct our care. It is genuine sharing on the part of those doing the caring. It is not our reaching down, but our reaching across. It is one drowning man with his arm around another, pointing to the Christ who has saved us both. One of the unique facts about the church in the city is the presence in many cases of the pastor and staff as part of the community in which they are involved. When I moved to East Harlem, along with half a dozen other clergy and our families, we discovered that we were literally the only professionals in the community of 215,000 people who lived in that neighborhood. We found no doctors, lawyers, social workers, or school teachers who shared their whole life with the neighborhood. Rather, they came in to "service" it on a contract basis. This relationship was obvious to the people in the community. Participation, on the other hand, points to an attempt to follow the pattern of incarnation. It also has a different ring than the word "identify." I cannot be black or Hispanic, but I may by the grace of God seek to participate with them fully.

B. *Relevance.* This overworked word is in contrast to the implicit problem of much caring which simply misses the mark or does not really do any significant good except perhaps for the welfare worker. An obvious sign of irrelevance appears when those whom we seek to help are caught in a cycle of repeated needs that is never broken. I remember a young social worker who spent five years working with gangs on the West Side. After a period in the army, he returned two years later to see the youngsters he had worked with now hardened criminals or junkies on the street corners. He was in very great anguish over the uselessness of what he had been about. What difference did his presence make?

Clearly, in seeking the welfare of the city, we can be quite irrelevant in terms of any significant impact. Years ago, Nicholas von Hoffman, then a lieutenant for Saul Alinsky and a key spokesman for the community organization movement, wrote an article called "Reorganization in the Casbah." There he attacked very harshly the social work establishment and the churches for the way in which they come into a community of need with their own preconceived programs of social service and set about doing good. They assume the roles of leadership because they are blind to any natural leadership which is operative in the areas where they are working. At the end of the year or two when the community has not shown much interest or gotten involved in their programs, they begin writing articles about the reality of apathy. They request twice as much money to double their programs in order to overcome the apathy of the community and to do it good. They fail to recognize, as van Hoffman suggested, that they really are trying to sell iceboxes to Eskimos. They have created programs that the community neither wants nor would benefit from, programs that have been imposed by those with a grim determination to help those in need. One shorthand way to put it is that it is far better to teach a man to fish than to continue to give him fish. But, of course, when that happens, the professional social worker or the professional do-gooder is out of a job.

C. *Effectiveness.* This factor offers up the necessary contrast to some efforts to seek the welfare of the city that actually do positive harm even as they generate some obvious good results. It is so easy to help a few while making matters worse for the many more. Some years ago, the narcotics scene on 100th Street between First and Second avenues became very grim. This center for a substantial amount of the drug traffic made life very difficult for the nearly four thousand people who lived on that one city block. The church, along with several other groups on the block, organized and then demanded of the local precinct that there be good police protection for a change. The consequence of this heavy pressure, quite unexpected and unusual in the neighborhood, led to twenty-four-hour police surveillance on East 100th Street. The result was the almost total dispersion of the junkies and a very unusual period of peace and quiet for 100th Street. But the result for the rest of East Harlem was total disaster. Junkies were able to operate with impunity in almost every other section of the community. Four thousand people benefited at the price of making life worse for a good many thousand more. We need to test our caring activities with this possibility in mind.

The same problem can emerge in a more complex way in something like a remedial reading program. The educational programs of our inner-city neighborhoods are by and large total disasters. The lack of any high expectations for children on the part of teachers only compounds the problems already facing the children. Many churches have developed remedial reading programs. They attract highly motivated children, almost always with parental support and encouragement. The results are often astonishing in terms of improvement in reading and, back when I.Q. tests were still being used, dramatic jumps in I.Q. level (which proves the phoniness of the tests, rather than the ability of the reading programs to change a child's I.Q.). But remedial reading programs have the potential of taking the heat off the public school system by providing an alternative for the children of parents who are likely to be active and angry about the failure of the educational system. Some have argued that it is better to give up the reading programs so that the energies of the parents and of those who run the programs might be directed toward improving the public school system rather than toward providing a safety valve for its failures. In any case, the test always must be: is the program genuinely creative or is it actually in the long run doing more harm than good? In aiding some, does it hurt many?

D. *Use of Facilities.* This mundane criterion is a way of reminding myself that no institution in the world is as profligate in the use of space as the church. The most affluent corporation uses its fancy boardroom more frequently than the church uses its expensive sanctuary. Elaborate Sunday school plants may be utilized for only an hour a week. If the church exists to seek the welfare of its community, then its facilities must be available as totally as possible to the community as well as to the church itself. The problems here are obvious in terms of feelings of danger to the property and all the rest, but as a principle we had better affirm strongly that we have been given the building to serve the community and not ourselves. Every opportunity for its use ought to be made available to the local neighborhood.

E. *Signs of Shalom.* In seeking the welfare of the city, pilgrims pray that they might be signs of shalom, hints of God's kingdom, the first fruits of God's promises. To be a sign of shalom is a matter not of intentionality, but of prayer and hopefulness, one of seeking to be in the way of the Holy

Spirit's action or standing in those places where one does see symbols of healing, love, and reconciliation occurring and affirming and supporting those symbols. It means that our signs of healing will not have any connotations of colonialism or imperialism. They will not be for the sake of getting new members or winning converts or taking scalps for Christ. Simply, we live in the style of our Lord: where there is hunger—seeking to feed, where there is sickness—seeking to heal, where there is loneliness—offering our love without any ulterior motive. Equally important, to be signs of shalom as part of the life of the church community often leads us to discover and meet unmet needs. In any community there are countless tasks which cry out for love and justice. But any person and any Christian community has only limited abilities and capacity. Are there particular tasks which it is our business uniquely to undertake?

I am persuaded that there is one very clear mandate for which no one else in our society seems to be responsible. Christians are called to look with open eyes and sensitive consciences at the community of which they are a part, seeking out those points of anguish, pain, sickness, and need that no one is noticing or paying any attention to. Our job is to discover those who have been forgotten, the problems that are ignored, the needs that have been unattended by the professional establishment—and there plant our flag of concern and do what we can to be a sign of love and hope.

I underline this point wih considerable emphasis, for it marks a very important point in the life of the East Harlem Protestant Parish. As clergy faced with the overwhelming problems of this inner-city neighborhood we went off in all directions, taking on innumerable challenges in the course of our early years. By the grace of God, a very wise retired college professor and administrator came to spend some time in the parish and made it his business to understand what we were about. Rather hesitantly he asked if we would mind if he were to write down some of his reflections. He told us we would not have to take them seriously, but he would be glad to share some thoughts he had. We were eager for what he had to say. The result was a quite remarkable paper called "Functional Integrity." (For a copy of this paper, write the author at 5 West 29th Street, New York, NY 10001.) He made a number of telling points, but one stands out. He remarked that we were trying to solve every social problem that came our way. We were, in his words, promiscuous do-gooders, seeking to love and care for everybody in a way that ended up being superficial and insignificant. He told us that the question must always be this, "Among all the good things that need to be done, what is the good that it is your business to undertake; that is, for which you have the resources of time, talent, and energy in order to make a difference?" We simply had to stop trying to put out every fire and succeeding nowhere for the sake of trying to really take care of a few fires. This question of functional integrity is a critical perspective from which any effort to seek the welfare of the city may rightly be viewed.

There are countless remarkable parables of congregations that have discovered new life and vitality in a caring ministry. There are many books on congregational renewal which have been written over the last twenty years. I want to end this chapter by listing a cross section of books which have been for me particularly helpful. I urge your reading some of them. I also list four basic books which have undergirded my own theological thinking about the nature of ministry and mission. Perhaps it is too strong a word to call them classics, but at least they have been for me critical in formulating my own understanding. And in rereading them, I discovered they still have a very considerable significance for today.

I. Classics in my understanding of the church and its mission:

Dietrich Bonhoeffer	*Life Together*
J. C. Hoekendijk	*The Church Inside Out*
H. Richard Niebuhr	*Christ and Culture*
Gibson Winter	*The New Creation as Metropolis*

II. Background books for church self-understanding:

Arnold B. Come	*Agents of Reconciliation*
James H. Cone	*God of the Oppressed*
J. G. Davies	*Worship and Mission*
Urban T. Holmes	*Ministry and Imagination*
Jose Miguez Bonino	*Doing Theology in a Revolutionary Situation*
William Stringfellow	*A Private and Public Faith*
Jim Wallis	*Agenda for Biblical People*

III. Studies of congregations in mission:

Roger Huber	*No Middle Ground*
Robert Hudnut	*Arousing the Sleeping Giant*
Jack W. Lundin	*Church for an Open Future*
Loren Mead	*New Hope for Congregations*
Elizabeth O'Connor	*Call to Commitment*
Melvin E. Schoonover	*Making All Things Human*
John Schramm	*Dance in Steps of Change*
Ernest Southcott	*The Parish Comes Alive*
George W. Webber	*The Congregation in Mission*

seek the shalom of the city: the prophetic task

Read Ephesians 6:10-20.

The Demand for a New Definition of the Prophetic

In this chapter I am concerned with the fundamental prophetic task of the Christian community. Clearly, any consideration of this topic needs to avoid the present misunderstanding and confusion that is inherent in most church life in the United States. Sometimes the prophet is defined as a cosmic fortuneteller. More often we use the term "prophetic" to refer to social action. The prophets were the many men and women in the more liberal denominations who were deeply involved in social action commitments during the 1960s, centered primarily in the civil rights movement, the war on poverty, and the protest against Vietnam. Today in such circles, there is often a residual disillusionment or discouragement about either the usefulness of such social action or the ability of the church to sustain it institutionally. There are a lot of scarred veterans around whose dreams of ending the terrible reality of racism in the United States or fighting a significant war on poverty have been badly shattered.

On the other side of the Christian community are those from more evangelical and pentecostal traditions that have always been hesitant of anything that smacks of "social gospel." This phrase as customarily understood in such circles is seen as antithetical to the Christian involvement in history. Once social gospel proponents occupied the turf of public involvement, many of our vital Christian communities on the evangelical side of the coin have not thought it proper to involve themselves in protest marches or significant political involvement. The prophet was one who denounced social evils but did not become involved in the dirty work of politics or social change. Members of these Christian communities could not find an appropriate biblical base for action. Of course, too many church members have supported (with enthusiasm) the structures which have made for racism, militarism, and poverty. Christians of all theological persuasions must find a fresh definition of their prophetic task.

The clue for this new understanding of the prophetic task of the church has arisen in recent years with a fresh emphasis on a basic New Testament concept, the reality of the principalities and powers. For those who have grown up in the liberal tradition, phrases like the "principalities and powers" and "the rulers of this present darkness" have been thoroughly uncongenial. From a scientific point of view they are useful only as interesting metaphors and are basically unreal and to be ignored. Now biblical scholars are providing a new interpretation that speaks to a wide spectrum of Christian traditions and can provide a new point of common concern for evangelicals, Pentecostals, and those from the variety of traditions expressed in mainline denominations.

When we examine a phrase like that in Ephesians 6:12, "For we are not contending against flesh and blood, but against the principalities, against the powers, against the world rulers of this present darkness, against the spiritual hosts of wickedness in the heavenly places," we have a basis for a dramatic understanding of the dynamic forces in our society. I have been much helped by Professor Walter Wink of Union Seminary, who reminds us that by principalities and powers Paul is talking about the basic structures through which human community and life are sustained. Humans, as we have noted earlier, are community-building animals. The basic structures of human life, the community-building and enabling institutions and ideologies, are what Wink defines biblically as principalities and powers. They are educational institutions, political parties, economic institutions, and structures. They are churches and social organizations. They include the American Medical Association, the Republican Party, the American Legion, and the Presbyterian Church. Just as human life is made in the image of God, so these structures necessary for human society are also given by God. Equally critical, like the individual who has discovered the power of his own self-centeredness (read "sin"), so, too, in the biblical understanding these structures are also fallen (read "sinful"). Like individuals, they stand in need of redemption. For me, this has become a powerful way of understanding the realities of our contemporary world with the pervasive power of evil expressed most grotesquely in the Holocaust and in our involvement in Vietnam. More important is my profound hope that we have a biblical basis by which to involve the energies of the evangelical churches, including many black and Hispanic communities, in a new consciousness of their prophetic vocation. Their resources are desperately needed in the prophetic task of challenging the principalities and powers and seeking to be signs of peace and justice in the world in which institutions as well as individuals need the witness of the gospel and signs of the kingdom.

I am particularly taken by the beginning of the verse which I have quoted above from Ephesians, where the author reminds us that we are not contending against flesh and blood. This again is a powerful way of affirming that in our prophetic struggle we are not called primarily to displace from positions of responsibility evil men, as though that would make a difference. One pervasive myth in American society is the assumption that an honest politician at the top can change the realities of the structures. This "lone ranger" myth of the individual hero who can single-handedly change the thrust of the structures has been contradicted innumerable times in the experience of American political life. An honest police commissioner in New York City can make an impact on his close associates, but his ability to deal with the "principality and power" of a police department as a social structure is incredibly limited. Our struggle at the time of Watergate was symbolized by Richard Nixon; but we were not fighting against flesh and blood, but the whole political structure in which the emergence of the forces which dominated Richard Nixon's life were inevitable expressions.

A basic form of principalities and powers is that of powerful myths which shape the thinking of American society or of influential members in it. When our basic ideals are not achieved, we inevitably deceive ourselves into thinking they are close to fulfillment when they are in fact "fallen." Firm expression of a New Testament understanding of principalities and powers would have led us far more quickly to recognize the facts of our involvement in Vietnam, our misappropriation of a disproportionate share of the world's resources, and our exploitation of Third World peoples, all in the name of freedom, democracy, and economic development. We would not have been surprised by Watergate if our understanding of sin had recognized its corporate expression in institutions and ideals and not seen it simply in individual terms. The biblical doctrine of the fall is the key to understanding of the alienation of the whole creation from God. It affects nations as well as persons.

We have allowed ourselves in many public areas an amazing degree of self-deception. This is a clear expression of what the Bible calls idolatry, the worship of idols.

The American public has developed an amazing capacity for tolerating contradiction; perhaps this is part of the price of domination. The ironies of it would be almost humorous were it not for the victims—those who suffer the consequences of American contradictions. The public grants extraordinary authority and power to the economic and political managers and gets, in exchange, unprecedented affluence and a protected sense of national pride and destiny. The nation is thus able to stay on top of the world heap and still hear its leaders continue to talk of our commitments to self-determination, freedom, and "peace with honor." The government is able to kill a million Indo-Chinese and justify it with: "saving them from communism," or "containing the Chinese theatre," or "protecting American lives," or "destroying a village to save it," or "not backing out of our commitments," or "bringing our prisoners home with their heads high," depending on the year of the war and the official administration line. The nation's leaders are exposed lying, cheating, and stealing while still keeping down the poor and repressing dissent to "preserve law and order." The United States is able to maintain two dozen dictatorships and still be the leader of the Free World. The American people are able to gobble up over half of the world's consumable resources and still "praise God from whom all blessings flow." (Jim Wallis, editorial, *The Post American*, Vol. 3, pp. 3 ff., now called *Sojourners*.)

The Prophetic Task for Christians

This understanding of principalities and powers as a very specific and concrete way of analyzing our human society and institutions leads directly to my understanding of the prophetic task of the church. The prophet in Israel, quite simply stated, was the "truth-teller." He was the person who sought to tell it like it is, to express in dramatic words and actions an understanding of the sinfulness of the nation in a way that would force Israel to recognize its grip by the power of the principalities and seek to recover a new faithfulness to the covenant with its God.

The prophetic task, in other words, has to do with unmasking the principalities and powers. It has to do with demythologizing, challenging the idolatry that allows us to be subject to the powers of institutions and ideals in a way that lets us compromise our commitments to Jesus Christ. Christians have made a strong commitment to Christian obedience as did the Jews in their covenant with Yahweh. The urgent task of our time is for the church to recover this prophetic ministry at the heart of its pilgrim vocation.

Unmasking the principalities and powers in the life of the Christian community may also lead us to challenge the powers of institutions by confrontation and serious encounter and by outlasting them as a powerful sign that they have ultimately no power over those whose life is lived in Christ. To this task we shall turn in the next chapter.

Paul writes in that remarkable passage in Romans 8:38-39, "For I am sure that neither death, nor life, nor angels, nor principalities, nor things present, nor things to come, nor powers, nor height, nor depth, nor anything else in all creation, will be able to separate us from the love of God, in Christ Jesus our Lord." This is the faith which empowers us for our prophetic task. In this chapter, I want to examine more specifically the biblical understanding of the prophetic task of unmasking and demythologizing the principalities and powers and then to examine several of the crucial myths which are so demonic in their hold over our society.

A. *Basic Components—Isaiah 58:1-9a.* Three Old Testament passages each provide a particular insight into the meaning of the prophetic task. The first is Isaiah 58:1-9a. (I hope the reader will have a look at it before proceeding.) Here is a basic prophet at work, crying aloud to Israel about its breaking of the covenant and its failure to recognize the reality of its own situation. Neither is this message fortunetelling, nor is it seeking to condemn the world outside the sanctuaries of Israel. The message is directed precisely to the household of faith. How easy it is for the prophet, thundering from the safety of his pulpit, to denounce the sins of those who are not present, as though they really cared about his words.

A simple illustration of this reality is found in Paul's first letter to the Corinthians, where he is discussing a serious problem of conduct in the church in Corinth. Apparently, a member had been involved in a serious moral problem and was unrepentant. Paul's advice is to throw him out of the church if, after admonitions, he still refused to repent. For the sake of the integrity of the household of faith and for the man's own well-being, it did no good to allow him to play games with his commitment. Paul ends this brief, but very heavy, passage on the need for strong discipline by reminding the congregation that its business is to judge its members and not the outside. That is God's business.

Would that the church would recognize that its prophetic function is initially within the household of faith and that it is God who judges the individuals in his world. "Cry aloud, spare not, lift up your voice like a trumpet; declare to my people their transgression, to the house of Jacob their sins." Is the task of Isaiah not unlike the work of Amos, Hosea, Micah, and others of the whole great prophetic tradition of Israel?

The urgency of this task for our own time is symbolized by

the incredible difficulty of getting straight any of the events of our day. In New York City, to have some clue about what is happening I find myself reading the *Amsterdam News* (the Harlem paper), the *Village Voice, The New York Daily News,* and *The New York Times.* The ability of these four journals to describe the same event in utterly different terms is a source of considerable amazement. To put it as directly as possible, Christians have been given the godly vocation of being those who seek to understand the events of their time and the realities of their own history in the perspective of God. They seek always to mitigate their own self-interest and distorted vision for the sake of helping all men and women see life with as much clarity and truth as can be achieved.

One further word about Isaiah 58. Note that this passage has a unique relevance for our own religious situation. The prophet was particularly disturbed because Israel at that point in its history, being somewhat affluent and at peace, was more religious than usual. Apparently, religious practices and attendance were on the upswing. Isaiah's point was that God was little interested in Israel's participation in religious institutions and activities. What cried out for attention were the problems of the poor, the dispossessed, the broken and needy people of that time. In effect, Isaiah is saying that God is deeply upset by religious participation that does not lead to sharing one's bread with the hungry, to bringing the homeless poor into one's house, to dealing with oppression in whatever forms it was found in Israel. This powerful passage provides us with a unique criterion for defining the integrity of our own institutional participation in Christian community.

B. *Prophetic stance—Isaiah 6:1-13.* This prophetic passage calls attention to the reality of the prophet's own involvement in the sin of the nation, in the grip of the principalities and powers that dominate his own people. "Woe is me! For I am lost; for I am a man of unclean lips and I dwell in the midst of a people of unclean lips; for mine eyes have seen the King, the Lord of hosts." (Read over Isaiah 6.) This passage has unlocked for me an understanding of my own distortion of the prophetic task during those active years of the 60s and 70s. It is what has been called the white liberal syndrome. The problems of the world clearly cried out for Christian involvement. Racism, poverty, the war in Vietnam, the breakdown of life in the cities—these were objective problems that were deeply impacting the life of many human beings. I thought it was the primary task of the Christian to try to help those who were the victims of these terribly oppressive situations. We who had the intelligence, the resources, and the freedom to help these less fortunate people had a God-given commitment to involve ourselves in doing something about their problems. Isaiah reminds those of us who sought to help others, without recognizing our own involvement in the problem, that *the issue begins with us* and not with the victims out there someplace. The problem in American society, in other words, is not black people, but white racism. The problem is not poor people, but those who are too affluent. The problem is not the victims of the war, but the unparalleled use of military might by the most powerful nation in the history of the world. In Bill Stringfellow's phrase, "My people is the enemy." I am one of them. "Woe is me . . . for I am a man of unclean lips and I dwell in the midst of a people of unclean lips."

The prophet is the person who deeply recognizes his own involvement in the sinfulness of his people and thus speaks from the midst of them, rather than over against them. Years ago, H. Richard Niebuhr remarked at a retreat that he had never preached a sermon with integrity unless, in a very real sense, he himself was sitting in the front row, equally under the judgment and encouragement of the word of God that he himself was proclaiming. The white liberal syndrome, in other words, is the white male seeking to help the victims of the structures which give him such an advantage in American life. It is my doing everything I can to help black men and women achieve greater educational, economic, and social advantages while I am continuing to benefit very happily from the racist structures, the principalities and powers that dominate American society. It is being very concerned about the problems of women's liberation while continuing to have many hidden advantages that come from the assumption of relationships in our society between men and women.

The concluding verses of the sixth chapter of Isaiah are also an important insight into the prophetic task, though ultimately very disconcerting. I have heard numerous sermons on the first eight verses of the chapter, ending with that remarkable call to Christian obedience, "Whom shall I send, and who will go for us? Then I said, 'Here am I, send me.' " What a great text for an ordination sermon or for the conclusion of a rousing call to social action. But Isaiah goes on in five concluding verses to remind the prophet that there is no reason to believe his message will be heard or taken seriously by the people. That does not, for one moment, give him the right to hesitate in his ministry or to draw back in despair. He is called to proclaim his vision of God's claim of justice, whatever may be the response. It is a salutary reminder that we are called to this prophetic task in season and out of season, with the task itself being the justification for our commitment, not any achieved results.

We may very well be in American life at a point in history when, to paraphrase Isaiah, the "hearts of this people have been made fat, their ears heavy and their eyes shut." As one reads over the great prophetic judgments in the Old Testament which remind Israel of the reasons for its unfaithfulness in its commitment to be a light to the nations, one is forced to recognize that our nation also is in the grip of the principalities and powers in a way that is utterly terrifying. The God of judgment is speaking to us. No nation in history has been as vulnerable to God's wrath as the United States today. Not because we are more evil than other nations, but because our self-deceptions are so powerful and our ability to force other nations to live under the burden of our idolatry is so overwhelming. Has any nation ever been quite as self-righteous in its use of political power around the world as we are? In Vietnam we killed a million people for the sake of democracy. In countless nations we support terrible military dictatorships in the name of democracy. In the name of development we have exploited Third World nations in a way that has increased the wealth of a few and extended the poverty of the many far beyond the situation before our development policy began. Yes, if there is a righteous God, I tremble for my people.

C. *The style of the prophet—II Samuel 11–12.* Look at the David/Nathan story in Second Samuel. The style of the prophet is beautifully expressed in this story from the life of David the king. You will recall that David, on the roof of his palace one day, sees a beautiful woman bathing several roofs away and decides that he would like to have her. As the story unfolds, David arranges for Uriah, the husband, to be killed in battle by the withdrawal of his support troops and then marries Bathsheba. The prophet Nathan hears about this and is called to action. Instead of our typical American pattern of writing a letter to the *Jerusalem Times* or denouncing the king in the pulpit, Nathan follows a much more effective pattern. He goes to see the king and begins by asking David about the nature of his kingship. Does David really believe in justice? Is he a king who rules under the power and direction of Yahweh? David answers emphatically "yes" to these questions. Well, says Nathan, you've got a problem in Israel. There is a serious question of injustice which is not resolved. David grows very righteous and declares that he'll set things straight. Nathan then tells him the story of the poor little shepherd who had only lamb that he deeply prized. When a rich landowner with all kinds of flocks has to prepare a feast, he takes the poor shepherd's only lamb and kills it. David is furious. He pounds the table and demands of Nathan, "Tell me who that person is; I'll make him suffer. There'll be no injustice like that in Israel." Nathan then replies in that classic statement, "Thou art the man." David was cut to the heart by the message of the prophet and repented.

Obviously there is no assurance that this will be the result of our preaching, but I do suggest that this David/Nathan story is a very helpful paradigm of what our prophetic task is all about. Our style demands that we have the wisdom and the cunning that might enable our words truly to penetrate our own participation in structures of injustice and even reach ears that are closed and eyes that are shut to the realities of the human predicament.

The urgency of this prophetic task comes in part from the present realities of our life in which no one else really feels the responsibility, with any seriousness, to tell it like it is. Unless one is deeply aware of the principalities and powers and seeks to compensate for their distorting power over our lives, even those who seek to be most objective in analyzing our human situation operate from clear perspectives and ideologies which are manmade and inevitably somewhat distorting.

One critical discovery of an educated person is that there

really is no clear right and wrong answer to the human situation, that the cry for love and justice is always in complex relationships which provide no simple solutions for their achievement. Those who are aware of the distorting power of the principalities and powers may seek the support of the Christian community and the power of the Holy Spirit to disabuse themselves of the power of their self-centeredness and try in every way they can to view the human predicament in the perspective of the Creator. The outpouring of books on Christian ethics indicates the complexity and difficulty of this task. I only argue for the need of the church to assume this prophetic role at a point when our society is filled with those who monger distortions and half-truths, when our television is a massive hustle seeking to peddle the products of an affluent society and when even our most prestigious newspapers often miserably distort or misinterpret the events of our time.

Crucial Areas for Prophetic Ministry:
Attacking Our Myths

A. *Democracy, and yet racism.* Just after the screening of the remarkable story of racism in America, *Roots*, I was with a group of clergy discussing its impact on the thinking of their people. Many of them indicated that it had a very powerful effect in revealing the depths of the reality of slavery, but that many of their people had said, "Thank goodness, that's in the past. Things are a lot better now." Our society as a major experiment in democracy for the whole of western history has always had a cancer at the very heart of its commitment. Slavery clearly could be tolerated only if the Negro was not really a full human being. Just as we had to make Vietnamese "gooks" and dehumanize the Japanese in World War II in order to engage in such massive killing, so the Negro, even in the Constitution of the United States, had to be declared only three-fifths of a man. The impact of the terrible institution of slavery thus was built into our society from the very beginning. It erupted in the violence of the Civil War and has continued to torment the integrity of our national life ever since. The domination of Congress by southern politicans with a decidedly conservative bent is a direct outcome of a one-party system created out of the period of Reconstruction and the impact of the Civil War. Myrdal put it accurately in 1944, when he titled his great book *An American Dilemma.* And the dilemma is still powerfully with us.

During my years at Union Theological Seminary, bordered as it was by Harlem, I became increasingly aware of the problem of Negro life in New York City and wrote a B.D. thesis on Negro protest groups in Harlem. It was thus with great hopefulness that we in the East Harlem Protestant Parish saw the emergence of the civil rights movement and became involved in this crusade. It was an exhilarating time beginning with the great Supreme Court decision in 1954 which declared that separate could not be equal. Then came the Montgomery bus boycott and the emergence of Martin Luther King as a leader of great stature and charisma, eventually to become winner of a Nobel Peace Prize and to be featured on the cover of *Time* magazine. There were the sit-ins in the South and then the great march on Washington culminating in civil rights legislation. Clearly, America was facing the challenge of this cancer in its very heart. The dilemma was being challenged, and we were making massive progress in overcoming the inherent evils of the days of slavery. Black men and women who had been locked in slavery for the first two hundred years and then left with little educational or economic opportunity after the Civil War were finally going to be brought into the mainstream of American life. America could resolve this problem.

And then, beginning in 1965, our cities erupted in those massive tantrums we called riots: violence directed against themselves by the suffering ghettos of our northern cities at first and then across the country. What had gone wrong? Again, we had been operating on the basis of a misunderstanding of the power of the principalities which are expressed in the structures of racism. White liberals had marched in Selma but had not faced the seriousness of the structures of racism, which are more covert and subtle in the North but far more powerful. Remember King's experience in Chicago when he sought to march through a white neighborhood. As he said at that time, "Those southern sheriffs ought to come up to Chicago if they want to learn really how to hate."

I have a very simple explanation for what happened in the violence in the North in those days in the inner-city black ghettos. For nearly a dozen years, the Negro community had been involved in a great civil rights revolution. The country was facing its problem and improvement was inevitable. But at the end of that period of time, the sociologists and economists took a look at the statistics and discovered that, true enough, on the social and economic indices the Negro community had been making progress in education, housing, income, jobs, and medical care; but at the same time, in those same years, the white community had made progress at a much faster rate. So the gap between black and white in American life had become greater precisely during those years of a "civil rights revolution." No wonder the Negro community said, "Who in heaven's name called this 'progress'? What kind of white trick has been played on us in convincing us that things were really changing when, in fact, the disparity in the races, the handicap under which we labor, has increased in these very years?" More important, the Negro community suddenly realized in a new way the danger of relying on the benevolence of their white liberal friends in achieving significant structural changes. White liberals, apparently, were not about to support the drastic changes in the basic structures of society which would really threaten the principalities and powers and make possible some new dimension of justice and peace. That is when the phrase "Black Power" suddenly emerged, a powerful rallying cry for a community which could now affirm for the first time its own identity and its authority. No longer would the black community be dependent upon its white allies or assume that their benevolence would be the route to the future. "Black" replaced "Negro" in our vocabulary. This vast illusion of how change takes place was shattered significantly at that point in history. Thank God for that unmasking of the principalities and powers.

Today the realities of racism are still powerfully with us in American society. While many black men and women who have had educational opportunities have been able to achieve significant positions in professions and business, the great mass of black men and women in this country still suffer under ever greater disabilities in terms of housing, medical care, education, and income. Our slums have grown more unlivable, not more humane, since 1954. In a sense, we are repeating the patterns of exploitation that have been the American pattern in other countries, where those who begin ahead in the race achieve greater power and wealth while the great mass of people during periods of development tend to be worse off than before. This is a sad reality for us all to face.

But even as the white community needs to recognize its own involvement in this tragedy, we may also be grateful for the signs of shalom which have emerged in the minority communities of our country. The self-understanding and the affirmation of identity by the black community is a great sign of its own recognition of the principalities and powers. "Black is beautiful" is a discovery of the power of one's own history. The black community does not suffer from many illusions these days. Many of those who have achieved positions of affluence and influence in our society recognize their own solidarity with their people in a way that challenges the old idolatry of the "black bourgeoisie." Above all, there is a vitality and commitment in many of the black churches which has grown out of the disillusionment with their relationship with the white denominations and churches.

B. *A word about other myths.* Just as racism is a powerful "principality and power" that effectively distorts American society and warps the integrity of our democracy, so other powerful myths are alive and well. For the present, these three might well be crucial areas for the prophetic task of the churches:

1. The assumption that all of American society is affluent when in fact we have a massive culture of poverty in which nearly 30 percent of our people are trapped with no effective means of access through education or jobs.

   Michael Harrington's passionate study, *The Other America,* is an authentic prophetic unmasking of this stark reality that most of us find almost impossible either to experience or to believe.

2. Myth of equality and the reality of sexism. The churches remain a strong bulwark of male privilege and domination in a culture that affirms equality for all

but continues to hold women, for the most part, in patterns of almost unconscious inferiority.

3. The myth of the good life in suburbia. The generation that fought World War II has made suburbia the synonym of the good life, leaving the cities to fester and burn. But the suburbs have not brought any guarantee of happiness or meaning to wives or children, and the breadwinner has paid a heavy price simply in commuting to uphold the myth. Principalities and powers are at work both in suburbia and in the city. The Christian in either place must live as exile and pilgrim, unmasking, demythologizing, and challenging them. As Heinrich Schlier writes in *Principalities and Powers in the New Testament* (Freiburg: Herder, 1961):

The members of the Church who have already been delivered from the principalities in Baptism in Jesus Christ must resist them the more strongly. Their aim must be to defeat the principalities in faith and loyalty, in works of justice and truth, in unceasing prayer, sober and vigilant, with the gift of the discernment of spirits. They must also endeavor through sacrifice to create in the Church a place free from their domination, as a sign of the new heaven and the new earth which are to come. (p. 68)

seek the shalom of the city: social change

There is one more essential element in what it means to seek the welfare of the city. So far, the specifics of that phrase "seek the welfare of the city" have involved an analysis of the community of faith as a place of nurture for exiles and pilgrims. A community gathered in Christ is by its very nature a political event. When men and women; young and old; rich and poor; educated and uneducated; black, Hispanic, and white gather at one table, it is a visible challenge to the principalities and powers which in our day deny the possibilities of that kind of community which breaks through the barriers of race, class and sex. The community of faith is also a challenge to the principalities and powers, to the normal ways of functioning in our world when it becomes a genuine caring community, caring not primarily for itself but for those in that community where God has placed it. To seek the welfare of the city also involves the fundamental, often overlooked, task of continuing the genuine prophetic ministry of the Old Testament tradition and of the ministry of Jesus. Exposing the myths, ideologies, and false structures of our society is a critical element in the ministry of God's people. But there is one further demanding task for the pilgrim community. This is to challenge and, wherever possible, to disarm the principalities and powers. This requires standing up against injustice and evil in confrontation even at the price of open conflict. This is the task usually referred to as "social action."

To Challenge and Disarm the Principalities and Powers

A. Realities for exiles and pilgrims. There are certain basic realities which must be taken clearly into account as the community reflects upon this urgent vocation. Let me list here facts which we dare not overlook if we are to undertake the task of political or public involvement in challenging directly the structures that have determined the realities of our contemporary society.

1. Willingness to face conflict. A great tragedy of the education in our churches is the picture presented of a Jesus meek and mild, gentle and loving, simply doing good by walking around the country of Palestine preaching and healing. What a shock then for children, and perhaps for all of us, when we come to the events of Holy Week and unexpectedly discover the hatred and passion with which Jesus is attacked by the political authorities of his day. Clearly, something had been mistaken in our understanding of Jesus. Suddenly it is clear that in his own life there is no separation between the private world of personal caring and the public world of involvement with the principalities and powers of his day, represented by the Roman soldiers and governor and by the religious leaders of the Jewish community. His presence and ministry clearly threaten to the core the powers of this world and lead them to bring him to the public humiliation of a death usually reserved for revolutionaries and common criminals. The fact that Jesus

in the wondrous event of the Resurrection triumphed so unambiguously over these powers is the very heart of the Christian confidence that we too dare live in the conflict situation with the powers whom Jesus so ruthlessly exposed in his triumph even over death.

A theory that embraces the necessity for conflict in the Christian life is easy to affirm but very hard to accept in one's own experience. I know full well that Christians inevitably are going to be in a fight, even if they operate with a totally nonviolent posture. Martin Luther King did not create violence in Chicago. The presence of a loving, gentle, nonviolent man simply exposed the hatred and passion of the forces of evil that were already present. They were exposed but not created. So it is with the Christian community. Even when it does not seek conflict, its very presence, if it is faithful to its Lord, will evoke hostility and opposition. In terms of the realities of this world, Christians are clearly troublemakers. In Acts there is the report to the authorities that the Christians had shown up in town; they are referred to as those "pests." Thus Christ calls us to accept and expect conflict as an essential part of our equipment for the warfare of God.

2. The congregation in most sociological situations is not a very helpful base for direct engagement in social change and conflict. When it comes to a direct challenge to principalities and powers, the sociology of middle-class congregations with its large contingent of passenger (nominally committed) members can hardly be expected to engage in serious controversy. This is not being cynical about the church, but simply realistic.

When God's people in our time seek to engage significantly in conflict with the principalities and powers, they almost certainly will need to find alternative structures to our normative patterns of residential congregations.

When a suburban church sets up a social action committee, time and time again the energy of the committee is spent in trying to convince reluctant church members they should be concerned about social problems that dominate the thinking of the committee. The incredible amount of energy that is thus dissipated in internal discussion and debate represents a victory for the devil. It neutralizes much of the potential energy of the members of the congregation who are prepared to undertake serious engagement with one or another of the principalities and powers. Those who are concerned about a particular problem should simply be set free to go about the task without expecting or demanding that the whole congregation should stand in support of their actions.

One of the most free-wheeling Roman Catholic priests in New York City, when asked how he got away with such radical social involvement, simply replied, "If I'm going to get the wrong answer, I don't ask the question." Or to put it another way, "I don't let the structures be a real problem for me. I'm a problem for the structures." There is a very real sense in which people like judicatory executives may in fact be grateful when men and women simply go ahead and take action in the public sector without asking permission of those in authority. Many a district superintendent has told me that he wishes his clergy would not ask for permission that he couldn't give from the point of view of institutional traditions and maintenance but would simply go ahead and take the risk of obedience to a higher will.

3. The complexity of social action. Involvement in conflict with the principalities and powers, with boards of education or the criminal justice system or the medical delivery system or narcotics addiction or racism or poverty or the military industrial establishment all present us with issues of such complexity and size that one's mind boggles

at the very prospect of any kind of significant impact or even clarity about where to enter the fray.

I suspect that a great deal of Christian "cross-bearing" is really the result of incompetence or naivete in the public sector rather than a genuine obedience. The Christian community needs the serious help of such sociologists and scholars as Andrew Greeley and Peter Berger, who continually challenge the naive and unsophisticated efforts of Christian "do-gooders" to make an impact in the public arena. But the fact is that our experts on the one hand and our institutional professionals, politicians, economic managers, and the like on the other hand have certainly given little effective wisdom in dealing with these great issues of our own time. The Christian brings into this arena one clear gift, that of an unambiguous commitment to human values.

This involves sensitivity to the impact of policy decisions on human life and a commitment always to challenge any programs or patterns which dehumanize men and women in the process of their achievement. It is this perspective which, if seriously present in the planning for low-income public housing projects, would have fought vigorously against the dehumanizing architecture of these vast new residential cities.

The complexity of the issues cries out for the use of the talents of Christian laity who provide the expertise to make our human commitments an effective reality. They also demand a recognition of the issue mentioned earlier, functional integrity. In a complex situation, the church in its forms and personnel will have to *pick its battles and its enemies* with some clarity and specificity. Amid all the good that needs to be done, what is the good for which we have the resources to engage in the battle?

4. The use of politics. Christians from a wide spectrum of theological positions and ecclesiastical traditions have been

chary about how, if at all, they might engage in the specific arena of electoral politics and government. Years ago, in his book called *Protestant and Catholic*, Kenneth Underwood analyzed the quite disparate ways by which the Roman Catholic Church sought to influence politicians in "paper city" by personal pressures while the Protestant community usually restorted to making policy statements that they insisted were nonpolitical in nature. When, for example, a strong statement was issued by the local ministerial association that was at once acclaimed by the local Democratic Party as clear support for their position, the Protestant ministers' group withdrew the statement. They clearly did not intend to support any political party by their pronouncement. This kind of naivete is not of much use.

For Christians in America, exiles in our style, we still remain citizens of this country with as much right to affirm our citizenship as Paul did in his work in the Roman Empire. As those who seek the welfare of our country, we have a profound obligation to make use of the potential creativity of democratic structures, whatever the degree of their "fallenness." One simple way to face the problem is this: when we do not participate, we always allow the status quo to continue without challenge. Not to act is to act in a way that sustains principalities and powers. When Jimmy Carter was running for election in the fall of 1976, Andrew Young at a board meeting of the National Urban Coalition was asked why Carter was paying so little attention to the cities. Young's response was direct. Recently, he said, in Bedford-Stuyvesant there was a bitter primary battle between Shirley Chisolm and a challenger for her seat in Congress. In spite of the importance of this election, less than 25 percent of the eligible voters bothered to go to the primaries to cast their ballots. Young said, with this kind of apathy in the inner cities there is little reason for Mr. Carter to give it priority in the heat of this election campaign. Precisely, the apathy of most voters does make it possible for a small group with a clear sense of commitment and direction to have an unexpected clout in the political structures of our day.

5. Perspective is crucial in challenging the powers. I have survived in a city by a personal text, "Try to be a significant drop in the bucket," as opposed to being simply an insignificant drop in the bucket. We are not called to defeat the powers but to challenge them wherever we can to disarm or cripple them, always in the recognition that ultimately it is our involvement in the battle that is our witness to the kingdom of God and that we are not dependent on ourselves winning the victory.

6. We are "humanitarians" for Christ's sake. In our challenge to the principalities and powers, our primary concern is not to convert men and women to Christ but to empower the powerless, to provide hope for those who live in despair, to restore sight to the blind, and to set at liberty those who are oppressed. I have long since stopped resenting it when people criticize the work of the church by claiming it is nothing but "humanitarianism," no different from what social workers would undertake. We have an understanding of what it means to be truly human, given to us in the life of Jesus. This understanding we affirm and seek to make possible for all men.

Let me give one example of what I mean. During the heated period of the civil rights struggle in the mid sixties, a major Roman Catholic seminary in the New York area held an all-day conference on "Ministry in the City." Since the student body contained no minority students, someone had the good sense to invite half a dozen black leaders from Bedford-Stuyvesant to be present at the conference as resource leaders and participants.

After dinner, there was an open forum for several hours with all the consultants, the whole seminary student body, and the faculty included. Early in the discussion, one student, typical of his generation, stood up and asked one of the panelists, a large black woman named Thelma, "Could you tell me what you think of the witness and ministry of the church in Bedford-Stuyvesant?" Her immediate response was, "The church is a total disaster. Christians there seem to care only about themselves and have no interest in the problems of the community or the issues in the neighborhood." She went on for several further minutes dumping all over the institution of the church as she knew it. Seminary students tend to like that kind of attitude about the church and applauded what she was saying. But my point is that over an hour later, after the same black woman had spoken about a number of other matters, one student was moved to say to her, "You are a very beautiful person, and I have been deeply moved by what you have to say. Is it fair to ask you how you got this way, so free to share your concern and so committed to the problems of Bedford-Stuyvesant?" She laughed and answered quite directly. "Sure, I don't mind. You should've seen me a couple of years ago. I was on welfare, livin' in a lousy rat-infested, stinking tenement on McDonough Street; I didn't have a nickle to go to the movies, I didn't care what happened to my kids, I wasn't livin' at all, I was just existin'.' One day a nice young priest came along and knocked on my door, and said, 'Thelma, this ain't no way to live. You gotta get involved. You gotta come with me to the welfare rights movement.' I told him, 'Sure, I'd come,' but I didn't mean it. He came back that night, however, and dragged me by the hand to that first meeting, and I've been going ever since."

In a traditional sense this story might be looked upon as

one of failure. Highly critical of the institutional church and not really involved, this woman had not been brought into his flock by the young priest. But from another point of view, is not this a story of death and resurrection? A woman with no sense of her own identity or history, simply existing in that lousy tenement, suddenly discovered that she had gifts and significance as a person and that she was needed in the struggle for justice for welfare mothers in the city. In discovering her identity and her vocation, she had become a beautiful and alive person. Though she did not accept the name of Christ in any conscious way, is it not possible that she had discovered the very meaning of humanity which those who know the name of Christ can affirm with gratitude? One goal was achieved in her life. She was now free to live responsibly and care for God's world.

B. New structures: some clues. Clearly, the congregations of our day are not the only base from which to move into the arena of direct confrontation with injustice. This is not a limiting reality but a way of suggesting that Christians are free to seek new wineskins, to look for a variety of ways in which we can shape structures that will be effective in our work far beyond the institutions of the moment. This is a tough time to make such an affirmation. During the sixties and early seventies there was a tremendous openness in the Protestant and Roman Catholic communities to generate new forms of witness and presence that would be para-parochial or ecumenical in their basis, providing a whole range of new missionary opportunities. Countless examples come to mind. In order to develop new programs in controversial areas of social change, the major denominations created an organization called IFCO (Interdenominational Foundation for Community Organization). Such an organization offered a way of funding controversial organizations through an instrument that did not directly implicate the denominational sources from which the funds came. During the early period of the Vietnam War, most denominations and congregations were certainly reluctant to look seriously at the implications of our U.S. involvement in what then was assumed to be a dirty, but necessary, war grown out of a humane concern for protecting the Vietnamese people against the menace of worldwide communism. A group of clergy and laity formed a new organization outside the traditional denominational structures called "Clergy and Laymen Concerned about Vietnam" (now "Clergy and Laity Concerned") to provide a vehicle through which those desiring to cry out against the injustices of that war could find a structure for their own involvement and effectiveness. Over the years, CALC has been, and still is, a remarkably vital conscience for the Christian community and a significant challenge to the principalities and powers which sought to misrepresent in such horrifying ways the reality of our involvement in Southeast Asia.

In the World Council publication that grew out of the missionary structure study called *The Church for Others*, there is a long discussion of new structures that emerged during the last ten to twelve years. The sad fact is that the retrenchment of denominational funds and the introversion of much of our church concern has seen the withering of many of these once promising alternative structures for public involvement. It is ironic, for example, that in the greatest industrial nation in the history of the world the movement called the Industrial Mission, beginning in Detroit and with other programs in Newark, New York, and Boston, among others, is an almost insignificant involvement of the church with the massive industrial enterprise. Yet these programs have been symbols of what might be new structures for the church's life. For the interested reader, there are a number of books and publications which describe these alternative missionary structures and provide a helpful picture of their work.

"And Pray to the Lord on Its Behalf"

Jesus reminds us that we should love our enemies. I have always suspected that this advice is given to us in part because it is the enemy that is more likely than our friends to tell us the truth about ourselves. Jeremiah had something much more profound in mind, as I'm sure did Jesus. Prayer for our enemies is a critical balance to our efforts to seek the welfare of the city. This important verse in Matthew 5 is a reminder to those involved in social action that a significant commitment to prayer is an equal and crucial ingredient in their pilgrim task, even as their challenge to seek the welfare of the city is a reminder to those who prefer the path of prayer that these two critical elements must go hand in hand. There are several obvious reasons why this is such a critical element for the Christian. For one thing, when we pray for the city, it may serve to remind us that we dare never dehumanize the individuals who are on the other side of the fence. How easy it is to focus our anger on Richard Nixon for all that Watergate involves, or on a corrupt politician, or on the evil president of a corporation when we have clear evidence in the New Testament that our warfare is not against flesh and blood but against principalities and powers. Individuals are victims of the principalities and powers, even though they may be vital instruments of their demonic activities. Our struggle is against the corruption of the political machinery, not against an individual. Our struggle is not against the individuals who sit in the seats of power. Only as we recognize this fact will we escape from the illusion that in replacing evil men with good we somehow will change the reality of the fallen principalities.

In the second place, our prayer for the welfare of the city helps keep the challenge clear. Prayer is a way of stoking the fires of memory and hope, so that we are clear about our calling, our style, and our commitments. It is the way we again focus our energies on the community of faith that provides the focus, specificity, and perspective which alone enable us to enter into our warfare with assurance. Prayer is a way of remembering whose we are and what we are called to be and do in his name. Look again at Ephesians 6:10-20, where the author outlines the armor of our warfare. It is in prayer that we polish again the breastplate of righteousness, remind ourselves that our feet are shod with the gospel of peace, and take up again the helmet of salvation and the sword of the spirit. It is in prayer that we are contantly reminded of the nature of our warfare and of the importance of the witness which we make in spite of the opposition which occurs.

I have been deeply impressed in recent days by the way in which the Hispanic community in New York City, out of a profound commitment to the spiritual discipline of prayer, has come also to discover that it faces the principalities and powers in our city and has every right as congregations of God's people to enter into the public arena in a new way. The formation of Accion Civica Evangelica among initially a wide-range of Pentecostal clergy and laity and now with many of the mainline Hispanic pastors also participating is a sign that this evangelical group has discovered that Jeremiah is right, that in seeking the welfare of the city and praising to the Lord on its behalf, they fulfill an authentic Christian obedience.

I am suddenly aware that there must be much more that needs to be said about this commitment to pray for the city.

Perhaps my own poverty of thought reflects something of the barrenness of one who is heavily involved in social action but who has discovered that this element of our life of faith is as critical as our actions. Certainly, I become suddenly mindful of the passage where Jesus reminds his disciples that certain demons can be cast out only with much prayer and fasting.

There is a sense in which, having done all we can through our actions, we are left with the possibility of offering our weaknesses and our hopes to God in prayer through Christ. That may have a power beyond our own imaginations. It was said about Dwight L. Moody that he worked as though it all depended upon Dwight L. Moody and prayed as though it all depended upon God. We have no right to leave it to God in prayer unless we have done all that we can in human terms. But having done all, then dare trust in God; for in his hands the verdict is already secure. When, in my struggle against sin, I grow weary, I am sometimes reminded that I have perhaps been trying to play God and have failed to realize that I can place my trust in him and need not in a compulsive puritan way continually exhaust myself in some frantic struggle to achieve the victory already won. In First Peter there is a remarkable word of advice to the early Christians.

> Beloved, do not be surprised at the fiery ordeal which comes upon you to prove you, as though something strange were happening to you. But rejoice in so far as you share Christ's sufferings, that you may also rejoice and be glad when his glory is revealed. If you are reproached for the name of Christ, you are blessed, because the spirit of glory and of God rests upon you. . . . Therefore let those who suffer according to God's will do right and entrust their souls to a faithful creator. (I Peter 4:12-19)

127

In our prayers we may be reminded that we dare to trust in God and that his faithfulness is everlasting.

"For in Its Shalom You Will Find Your Shalom"

Jeremiah, in a dramatic foreshadowing of the reality demonstrated so vividly by the life of Christ, reminds the exiles that in seeking the welfare of the city and praying to the Lord on its behalf they discover the meaning of their own lives. It is in losing their lives for the sake of Babylon that they discover the joy of their full humanity. Is this not precisely the experience of all those who have been liberated from self-centeredness by Christ and have thus discovered that in caring with him for his world and sharing in his ministry they discover a joy in life beyond their own imaginations? It is not a ridiculous, but a profound, wisdom that reminds the exiles to seek the welfare of their oppressors.

A very sensitive black historian told a group of us once in the course of a discussion about black/white relationships that, for better or for worse, the black community was stuck with having to live in a household that was largely white. There was no way to escape from that reality. The tragedy, he affirmed, was the potent ideology of the white community that spoke about the melting pot. For when blacks were put into the melting pot, they were supposed to end up white. He said that for our survival together a far better metaphor was that of a salad bowl in which the various ingredients would maintain their own identity but together would make for a wholesome dish. In a sense, the Christian community is stuck with being part of the society where it finds itself. The radical sectarian option simply is not available if we are to fulfill our mandate. But we can seek to be ingredients in a mixture that will create a more humane community for all. We discover our own full humanity when we participate in Christ's mission for all humanity.

For me, a contemporary hero, one in whom the spirit of Jesus seems somehow uniquely captured, is Cesar Chavez, leader of the United Farm Workers of America. In a class at Union Seminary, Chris Hartmire, who has been for many years director of the California Migrant Ministry, a program of the churches to support the Farmworkers, was describing his experience with Chavez. He reminded us that to be with Chavez must be something like the experience men and women had with Jesus. The power of his presence and charisma meant that you had to either accept or reject him; you could not be neutral. Many people in Chavez's presence find themselves angry or hostile or simply put off and turn away, while others, like Chris Hartmire, find an experience of power and beauty. We asked Hartmire what it was that made Chavez like this. His response was very direct. He said that as a young man Chavez had taken some time out (forty days in the wilderness) in order to get a grip on his own identity and sense of what is important in life. He discovered that he could affirm his identity as a Mexican-American and that he had gifts which were important. He decided that what would make his life worth living would be in Hartmire's words "to take my life and use it for others." Without any theological sophistication, Chavez had discovered his own identity and his own sense of vocation in a way that Christians can affirm as a sign of God's grace. Chavez has somewhere written:

> When we are really honest with ourselves we must admit that our lives are all that really belong to us. So it is how we use our lives that determines what kind of men we are. It is my deepest belief that only in giving our lives do we find life. I am convinced that the truest act of courage, the strongest act of

129

manliness, is to sacrifice ourselves for others in a totally nonviolent struggle for justice. To be a man is to suffer for others. God help us to be men.

Here is a man whose life expresses his self-understanding and his commitment. My only quarrel with this statement, apart from the sexist language which is perhaps excusable in the light of the date when that statement was written, is the use of the word "sacrifice." This is so loaded with overtones of false martyrdom and stiff upper lip self-righteousness that I would just as soon eliminate it. It is not exactly sacrifice when by seeking obedience one discovers the joy of life. It is an undergirding of the words in Hebrews 12, where it is reported that Jesus, for the joy that was set before him, endured the cross, despising the shame. This is a little different use of the word sacrifice than in our common parlance.

In the end, there is no way to convince by any arguments that we do discover life in seeking the welfare of the place where God has placed us. The only way I know to authenticate the Christian insights is try it. Ultimately, the Christian faith makes sense out of the experiences we have already discovered to be authentic. It becomes a way of understanding what we somehow know to be true, "Try it, you'll like it."

matters of strategy for exiles & pilgrims

Read I Corinthians 12–13.

Clergy and Laity: Appropriate Interaction

From the discussions of the life of the exile community and its vocation in seeking the shalom of the city, there are strategic implications which are important to pursue, clues which suggest emphases and areas that need attention. What might happen if congregations as presently organized were to seek to accept this new sense of identity and to grow in seriousness in their vocation of seeking the welfare of that community where God has placed them for witness and service?

In the early years of the study program of the World Council of Churches, a very creative effort came from the department of the laity. Under the leadership of Hans-Ruedi Weber, a new sense of the importance of laity as the critical personnel in the life of the church began to take shape. Basing their new emphasis on serious biblical study, the department of the laity sought to overcome the almost universal pattern of clergy as the professional with the laity functioning as assistants rather than as partners in the community of faith. The work of Hans-Ruedi Weber was given substantial undergirding by important books—the first by Hendrik Kraemer on *A Theology for the Laity* and then a massive theological study by a Roman Catholic priest, Yves Congar, called *Lay People in the Church*. The most useful study for the congregation continues to be the book by Arnold Come, *Agents of Reconciliation*.

Most younger clergy have been thoroughly indoctrinated with the importance of lay leadership and are quite articulate in proclaiming the importance of the laity in the life of the congregation.

But the fact remains that this strong new theological emphasis has had little obvious effect in most congregations. This is due partly to the power of our rituals which convey a meaning quite opposite to what we may declare with our fine sermons. For example, in the Presbyterian tradition, ruling elders are ordained and vested with authority just as the clergyperson. But the ordination service for the elders is usually during a brief section of a regular Sunday liturgy while the ordination of the teaching elder (the pastor) is at a formal service of the presbytery with great pomp and regalia, usually several hours in length. The service both honors and challenges the young person to all the multiple responsibilities that alone are claimed to fall upon the clergy. The symbolism of this is all too obvious to any of the members in the church.

It is also much too easy for clergy to affirm the importance of the laity and yet to continue in much the same way to operate in the traditional roles for which they have been trained and to which they have been assigned. Theological seminaries continue to stress four basic areas in which clergy competence is essential: preaching, teaching, counseling, and administration. They are roles which the pastor must learn to fulfill, but I have difficulty with the use of the word "role." I find myself reluctant to use this expression any longer, because it suggests an actor in a play, a part to be lived out, a costume to be worn, rather than the clergyperson's assuming functions that grow out of a common Christian commitment and are expressed by a living person, not a professional. Role or function, person or professional, the distinctions are a source of very serious tension that goes beyond semantics. Clearly, a clergyperson is a professional in many of the traditional understandings of the word. Several good recent books have been written underlining the fact that the clergy are professionals. They are given specific training, expected to have certain competencies, and are part of a structure for which there are particular requirements.

On the other hand, there is a very obvious difference between clergy and other normative professions. Their identity as persons is more confusing for clergy than for other professionals. A doctor can be a doctor, but when he goes out to play golf, he can be a golfer. But for clergy, their personal and professional roles are seen as inextricably locked. Or put it this way: as a clergyman I ought to be competent, but I don't want to be professionalized. It is difficult to live with this tension when one looks at all the expectations that are loaded on the clergyperson.

The issue for clergy is to be human, to be authentically themselves, and yet to be competent where competency is required. This is the tension between the professional competence that is required in their function within the congregation and the necessity of being encountered by men and women of the parish as an authentic human being. Whatever our ecclesiastical traditions, there is no biblical basis on which the clergy can opt for a professional model. The ministry of Christ was given to the congregation. It is the clergy's function within that context not to be the center of the show, the mother of the family, but to find a way of embodying a serving ministry for the whole people of God. The model is not that of the authority of the risen Christ but of the servanthood with which Jesus related to his own followers. It is very difficult for clergy to go through the process of education, accreditation, and ordination and still recognize in themselves that they must live with an incarnational faith. It is even more difficult for their congregations to accept that reality. But I suggest there is no other way for a congregation to be seriously engaged in its vocation as long as the center of its life is the clergyperson. His/her task must always be primarily within the gathered life of the church. The clergy inevitably tend to stress activities that relate to the functions where the congregation gathers for its mission of nurture rather than those of engagement in seeking the welfare of the community.

The way ahead must recover in all its power a biblical understanding of the variety of gifts, often in Protestant circles referred to as "the priesthood of all believers." Luther, in his stress on this doctrine, did not for one moment try to eliminate the functional responsibilities of clergy. What he did seek to do was to stress the central importance of the laity's using their variety of gifts wherever the Holy Spirit was at work. In First Corinthians 12, as in the passage we examined in Chapter 4 (Ephesians 4:11-16), Paul makes clear that the congregation is a body with a variety of parts and with a variety of gifts. The health of the whole depends upon each part's working properly, with each gift being accepted, disciplined, and utilized. It is the clergy's responsibility to assist the overall functioning of the body, but clearly the clergy cannot expect to possess or exercise in any primary way each of the variety of gifts which are given to the many members.

A way of underlining the meaning of the priesthood of all believers is to stress the importance of a congregation's being a team of ministers with the clergyperson being one member of that team. Perhaps the only distinction is that he or she can give full time to the particular functions properly assigned to the clergy's portfolio. Then there is some hope that all gifts of God's people might be discovered and utilized.

At New York Theological Seminary, in our doctorate of ministry program, no student is allowed to proceed beyond the initial stages until that student is able to demonstrate that in the parish setting a ministry team is being established in which a genuine sense of mutuality in ministry and corporate responsibility becomes the mark of that congregation's life. In the setting of a team ministry, then, the traditional functions that have been the critical role models for the clergy can take on quite different shape.

A. *Preaching.* The essential task of preaching is to break open the Scriptures to men and women of faith. Traditionally, the Protestant method has been to read a passage from the Bible and then to expound on it for somewhere between ten and sixty minutes, depending on the pattern of the denomination and the style of the clergy. Preaching is designed to edify, inspire, and direct, to clarify our commitment to Jesus, and to direct our obedience.

Today these purposes are far more readily achieved for many in a more dialogical setting where Bible study is the context of preaching. Here the goals of preaching can be achieved in a corporate process not unlike the dialogue that ensued in the synagogue in Nazareth, where, after Jesus had stood up to read Isaiah 16, he sat down and led a discussion of what he had read (Luke 4:16-21). When a congregation starts out with an initial low level of biblical literacy, the way ahead may well be the establishment of cell groups or small communities of faith for regular Bible study. It's an easy step to relate the Bible study directly to the sermon which will be preached on the following Sunday. Thus, when the minister preaches in the Sunday morning setting, there can be reliance upon the study and biblical recognition for those who have been involved in the study groups. The discussions which have occurred in the parish during the week on that passage can also help in significant ways to direct the actual content. Many congregations discover that preaching from a pulpit becomes far less vital and effective than preaching experienced in a setting in which a more dialogical style of communication can be expressed. In effect, God's people—clergy and laity— gather before an open Bible and together seek, with the particular guidance of the clergy, to hear what God is saying to them. Thus, as Richard Niebuhr expressed, the clergyperson is always as much a part of the congregation to which the word is addressed as the instrument through which it is spoken in that particular setting.

B. *Teaching*. The teaching function now becomes much more than a clergyperson's relating the content of the faith; rather, teaching has to do with the opportunities for growth in the Christian life, the pedagogy of which was discussed in an earlier chapter. It has to do with the urgency of preparation for pilgrim tasks. If we "do not know what we do not do," then significant education always is an effort to understand and strategize in terms of the particular areas in which we must be making significant decisions.

The model here, above all else, is that of "doing theology." This requires us to develop the ability to bring the resources and perspective of our faith into a living interaction with the decisions, commitments, and engagements where we are putting our own life energies.

Here is one illustration of an exercise in "doing theology." Sit down regularly with a group of men and women. Ask one person to bring to the group's attention an article of importance that has appeared in the newspaper during the last week, one in which he or she had some personal involvement or stake. First, ask the group to look for the biblical and theological resources which will provide perspective in interpreting and understanding the events that are taking place in God's world. Secondly, search for faith resources which help to decide what actions are appropriate. "Doing theology" demands both involvement in the events or situations and ever deepening understanding of the resources which God has given us in the events of the old and new Israel.

C. *Pastoral functions.* In a team ministry, the clergy and laity can work at that massive breakthrough which is required if the traditional members of the congregation are ever to accept the fact that they are part of the priesthood of all believers, in which gifts of caring and even of personal counseling can be found often far more effectively in members of the congregation other than the clergyperson. It is a caring community which fulfills the pastoral function, rather than a caring parson.

D. *Administration.* Important is the broad use of administrative gifts which are inherent in the experience of many laity. As important as administration is, it also needs to be said that every session of a committee or board can be an occasion for nurture and ministry. When committees deal only with business matters, they easily forget their relationship to the function of the congregation. Institutional maintenance quickly dominates the sense of vocation and purpose. In the whole administrative area, there must be a sense of nurture and preparation. Maintenance must be instrumental and not decisive in its own right.

As I reflect on the functions of the clergy, two terms come to mind which seem to express the various dimensions of the task. The first is "rabbi." As preacher and teacher, the task of the clergy is to enable men and women to grow in faith, to nurture their lives in Christ. This is the traditional rabbinic function. When William Sloan Coffin was installed as pastor at the Riverside Church in November, 1977, he was challenged to be a rabbi, to test the faithfulness of his ministry not by the power of his sermons or the charisma of his teaching but by the degree to which the men and women of his congregation grew toward maturity in Christ under the leadership of their rabbi.

But he was also challenged to accept a second conception of his ministry, this time a secular one. He was told to let his pastoral and social action concerns fall under the designation of "community organizer." The clergyperson, like the kind of organizer defined by Saul Alinsky and the community organization movements of our time, is the one who operates behind the scenes, empowering the natural leadership of the community, doing the necessary work of maintenance and preparation, becoming significantly involved in a very personal way in the goals and tasks of the organization; but the clergy person is not the one who either takes aggressive leadership or gets credit for what develops. Some years ago, a national magazine did an article about the work of "Metro-North" in East Harlem. It was a very competent and thorough article describing an impressive community action program, but the author completely missed the fact that behind the scenes was a clergyman who had lived and worked in that community for nearly twenty years. His relationships, know-how, and sensitivity had been a critical enabling factor in the cohesion of Metro-North. The fact that the reporter overlooked this important role is a wonderful indication of the superb competence with which this clergyperson had functioned as a community organizer for Metro-North. Reflect on that possible style for the clergyperson in a congregation today. The job description then makes use of such verbs as releasing, empowering, equipping, challenging, serving.

In writing this chapter, I came across an old article I had written a good many years ago about the task of theological education. In it I had stressed three basic qualities or traits which are important for clergy. As I read over those words, I am now convinced that the same three characteristics or qualities are precisely required not for clergy alone, for for all of God's people called to their own ministry, for all Christian men and women.

The first trait is that of a *worldly person*. That is to say, men and women must have freedom to function as responsible human beings in the modern world. The sad fact is that for many of our clergy and Christian laity, the world in which their faith is exercised has been a protected milieu, often disengaged from the areas of life where they must make significant political and economic decisions. Often, those who are most involved in the life of the church have expressed their faith only in the protected relationships of the church rather than subjecting it to the rough challenge of the contemporary world. Seminary students, for example, are likely to have made a decision to seek ordination in the high school youth group and been involved all the way through their academic preparation in religious organizations rather than having to struggle with the give and take of secular involvements. The Christian is one able to live with the freedom of the Incarnation, as did Jesus, sharing fully in the life of the world, going, in Auden's phrase, "native in all things, save faith and morals."

The second trait of the Christian obviously, is to be *a person in Christ*, to work always toward the maturity of the fullness of the stature of our Lord. My point here is that many find it easy to be a worldly person, and many seek to be recreated in Christ; but it is the combination of these two that is expressive of a commitment based on incarnation. These traits are not mutually contradictory, but dialectically essential. The exciting thing about the man Jesus was that he took the Incarnation seriously. He lived as a free man in the world. He joined in weddings; he even turned water into wine. He wept with those who grieved. He was committed to responsibility as a man of the world. He did not spend much time in church or with church people. He faced the challenge of a society that did not take his presuppositions for granted and whose language he had to learn to speak. But at the same time he was a man of profound faith who was free to live in the world because of the kind of disciplined life which left him always dependent upon the grace of God. In the exile community, the Christian, whether clergy or laity, must be involved in a disciplined community of mutual commitment, like that between Jesus and his disciples. No one alone can find either the perspective, strength, or self-criticism which will enable one to function responsibly as a Christian. Only in a community of reflection, where we learn to speak the truth in love with our own peers and to bear one another's burdens, will we be able to live in the tension of a radically changing world which throughout our ministries will continually demand a rethinking not only of the structure of the church but of the gospel itself.

The third trait, for clergy and laity alike, is that of *theological competence*. While the clergy may be given the time to become expert and disciplined in the theological resources of our faith, the ability to think theologically in the sense in which we have defined it demands both knowledge of scripture and tradition and a deep involvement in the life of the world. The clergy can provide resources for one side of the dialogue; but, clearly, laity are critical in providing from their own experience the other. Together clergy and laity may pray to become theologically expert in relating faith and life in a biblical way. It has been far too easy for clergy to learn to think theologically about theology and biblically about the Bible without ever having used their theological education as a basis by which to understand what it is that God is calling men and women to be and to do in the world where God is at work ahead of us all. The task of "doing theology," of significant theological reflection in faith and obedience, demands the gifts of both laity and clergy in a genuine partnership. Thus, the Christian is a worldly person whose life is shaped by Christ and who brings to contemporary history the ability to see all events in the perspective of God; that is, to think theologically.

The Necessity of Intervention

The second important area of concern, to me the most vital clue for congregational development, grows out of the experience of Project Test Pattern, in which the importance of significant outside intervention in the life of a congregation emerged as a key to vitality and renewal. Project Test Pattern grew out of the frustration of the Episcopal Church after twenty-five years of struggling to achieve congregational renewal. Loren Mead, an Episcopal priest, was asked to look for any further clues that might have been overlooked in the various renewal programs. After a year of exploring various alternatives, Project Test Pattern stumbled upon a very simple, but critical, factor. It discovered that when the dynamics for change, renewal, redirection in a congregation are initiated by the clergyperson, they are fundamentally dysfunctional.

At this point conventional wisdom about the clergy's role

as dynamic leader goes out the window. When the clergy use their authority to demand change, it forces laity simply to do what the pastor wants without buying into the new plan, to resist with considerable strength, or to find other ways of ignoring or subverting the new ideas which the pastor seeks to impose. In a sense, the congregation may react as adolescents to the authority of a parent. Very few clergy have been successful in initiating change either significant or permanent in a congregation when they have been the basic source of the dynamics at work.

Project Test Pattern suggested a very simple alternative. Make use of a consultant, responsible to and owned by neither the clergyperson nor the laity, rather someone whose first and primary task is to help create the kind of team ministry I discussed in the previous section on clergy/laity interaction. An outside consultant can help create integrity in communication between pastor and laity. One goal is to reach a point where both begin to use the expression "we" in reflecting on the life of the church. The outside consultant is useful in helping the congregation and pastor together to examine the problems that the congregation faces, to look at what they wish to accomplish in the way of goals, and in general, to develop a corporate strategy that makes change possible, a strategy imposed by neither clergy nor laity but by what they discover together. They seek to implement these goals by uncovering and empowering the variety of gifts of ministry which are inherent in their organization.

The way in which intervention can be critical is described in both Loren Mead's little book, *New Hope for Congregations*, and in a casebook by Elise Desportes, *Congregations in Change*. They have fully persuaded me that intervention must be a normative pattern in the life of any congregation that is seeking integrity. Equally important, it can be done without excessive cost. This is a quite startling idea for both clergy and congregations. In the past, intervention has taken place only in times of crisis. It has been a sign of serious trouble when one resorts to intervention rather than to a normal resource for health and strength. In creating a new freedom of communication and mutual sharing, a consultant can be invaluable.

The second important role of the consultant is enabling a significant planning process to take place. When I came to New York Theological Seminary as president, it was at a time of considerable crisis in the institution. My arrival was a source of very great concern to the ten members of the faculty who were unsure what kind of drastic changes might be required and nervous about the authority style of the new president. One of the faculty members, who also had a substantial outside commitment as a psychoanalyst, suggested to his colleagues that we ought to go away for a three-day retreat to get acquainted with the new president. A clergyperson who has considerable skills as a consultant was asked to join us. During a remarkable period of three days the president became simply a member of the group. In honest dialogue the faculty's fears and the president's concerns were shared and a new set of relationships began to emerge. Equally important, it was discovered that among the members of the faculty there were more than a few sources of anger, resentment, and misunderstanding that also could appropriately be ironed out in that context.

In the congregation, inevitably, the same need and possibility for open honest communication, for speaking the truth in love exist in order to grow both in faith and obedience. Again and again, in the D.Min. program at New York Seminary, the clergy set about creating a team ministry with great reluctance and hesitation. It hardly matters at all from what ecclesiastical tradition the pastor comes. In all of them, whatever the theory, the clergyperson is the dominant figure in the congregation. The idea of a team ministry among clergy and laity sounds attractive, but when the time has come to form it, the resistances are almost always massive. But as the process unfolds, as the laity discover that the pastor can take the truth, spoken in love, that he/she grows from honest feedback, the atmosphere changes. The pastor suddenly discovers that very powerful resources for ministry are being released among the laity and a new vitality enriches the whole parish. The clergy in the D.Min. program have testified over and again that forcing them to develop a ministering team is the most valuable part of the whole program. This subtle intervention of the seminary has been a critical factor in parish renewal.

The Planning Process

Using intervening personnel in addition to establishing open communication and creating a new sense of partnership can be an important step in creating an effective parish process. Planning is often a vital step that will enable a congregation to act from a sense of growing faithfulness in fulfilling God's calling. The moment one talks, however, about the planning process or goal setting in the context of the Christian community a lot of red flags go up in people's minds. It sounds like limiting the power of the Holy Spirit or imposing hard business models on an institution which operates with other ground rules. Of course, these warnings are sometimes appropriate, but we have this treasure in earthen vessels. The structures which are necessary to the Christian community do not operate under a different set of rules than other institutions. They are clearly subject to the same institutional patterns, now in the service of God rather than of mammon. A book far too little read, but of continuing importance, was written a good many years ago by Professor James Gustafson. *Treasure in Earthen Vessels* explores very systematically the way in which the church is both an institution with the uniqueness of God and an institution with realities that can be defined by the sociology of institutions.

I once had a phone call from a major foundation executive who had just spent a frustrating afternoon with several young clergy seeking a grant. He said that he had pressed them hard on how at the end of a year or two years, were he to give them the money they sought, he would know whether or not they had been successful. They told him that on theological grounds this was an utterly inappropriate question. They were called to faithfulness and not to success. He said that he then pressed them to learn how they would know at the end of a year or two whether or not they had been faithful and got no further satisfaction. They simply were unwilling, he said, to face this kind of question. What, he wanted to know, did I think about it.

The answer, I think, is that we have a desperate need in the church for planning that is clear and specific yet leaves open the movement of the Holy Spirit. We need to be clear about the goals toward which we are moving in our life and our work together. Faithfulness requires us to build into our programs significant feedback and evaluation mechanisms that force us to be hardheaded and honest about what is happening in the life of the community of faith. Once we identify ourselves as exiles and pilgrims, it takes no complicted statistics or professional evaluator to tell us if we are growing as individuals and as congregations toward maturity in Christ and in faithfulness in caring for the city. We have a ready set of criteria for our priorities and our programs: do they enable us to grow in faith and do they equip us for mission?

All kinds of manuals for church planning have been written by the denominations. The best single article I have come across was prepared by Dr. Robert Bonthius called "So . . . you want to change the system?" (written for Clergy and Laity Concerned, National Organizing Conference, Ann Arbor, Michigan. August 17, 1971). Although written specifically for an action group seeking to make some significant impact on a public program, its basic analysis is certainly helpful to a pressure group intent on change; that is to say, for any congregation.

The concept of success is clearly a paradox in Christian life. To live in conformity with Christ's life, to express in some partial degree his identity in our own lives, and to share in his ministry is more a matter of faithfulness. It reflects the discovery of joy, the establishment of coherence in our own lives between what God has called us to be and what we in fact are doing. Yet passages like the conclusions of Isaiah 6 give us no assurances of any kind of success in the task which God gives us other than the confidence that we are doing his will and living in a way that expresses his love. One need look only at a death on a cross to realize that biblically, the promises are of conflict with the principalities of this world, the expectation of struggle and pain. We are always surprised when there is joy and reconciliation and love as gifts that come to us in our life's journey.

In a somewhat different vein, the joy of the gospel is the promise that it is available to all men and women. In First Corinthians, Paul argues that the greatest gift is that of love. The exciting discovery, of course, is that the gift of love is no respecter of persons. No matter what the color of one's skin, black, white, yellow, or brown, whether rich or poor, educated or uneducated, God can grant the gift of love that breaks through all the human divisions and barriers that men and women have established in our world.

What is it that we may rightfully use as criteria for ultimate evaluation, for judging the appropriateness of who we are and what we are doing? The simplest way I know is to say that we must express as individuals and as communities of faith the three elements of Jesus' own ministry. The first element is that of community. The church must be a community of caring, of koinonia, where men and women may discover that in Christ there is neither male nor female, rich nor poor, Hispanic, black nor white; but in him these barriers are transcended and we are members one of another, a family of faith. When this reality is growing, we may rejoice in God's gift.

The second element is that of continuing Christ's ministry of servanthood, of healing and caring, a challenge to the principalities and powers, of the search for justice and peace. The New Testament word is "diakonia." Are we in the congregation continuing the servant ministry of our Lord not primarily for ourselves but for the people of God's world, entering into their lives as Jesus entered into the life of his community? Are we truly seeking the welfare of the city—wherever God has placed us for that kind of diakonia?

The third biblical word is "kerygma," or proclamation. Jesus came proclaiming the good news of the kingdom. So often, as men and women emphasize the fact that the gospel is about conversion, they fly completely in the face of the fact that Jesus came as an announcer. He came to tell the world that the kingdom of God was now at hand. The possibility was now. It was a reality into which men and women could enter with meaning and power. They could share in the first fruits of the kingdom. This was not a hardhanded pitch for conversion but an announcement to which men and women would have to respond in their own manner either to ignore or reject or accept. It is my firm belief that then in our day the church is expressive of

147

koinonia and when the congregation is about the task of diakonia, then we will be given countless opportunities to announce, to proclaim, to gossip with those around us about the meaning of the gospel. The presence of koinonia and diakonia is a sign that the kingdom is at hand and all are welcome to participate in its life and to march with those who accept the necessity of being exiles and pilgrims inspired by a kingdom whose full reality is not yet visible to all. Yes, I am persuaded that proclamation must always be preceded in our world, at this point in history, by the demonstration of the gospel through koinonia and diakonia.

How else might we look for indications that the congregation is being faithful? It occurs to me that one way would be to look for signs of shalom in God's world. Where are there reconciliation, love, healing, and justice? Then we place ourselves alongside them as those who affirm the power of Christ at work in the world. Sometimes I have thought that one way of judging the integrity of God's people was simply this: Are the people whom I find at the points of human need, where justice is being fought for, where love is being expressed, where there are these signs of the kingdom some of the same people with whom I gather around the communion table on Sunday morning? Are we offering our bodies as a living sacrifice where God is at work?

And, finally, there is a sense in which we know in the depths of our beings that we are in the right place, the right fight. Once at the end of a Bible study group, a member said, "Gosh, something is happening to us, isn't it?" The intuitive feeling of being in tune with Christ can sometimes be trusted.

epilogue: we live by hope

In this book, "exiles" and "pilgrims" have been two key words used to describe the life of the Christian community: exiles in the sense of one's own self-understanding, both for individuals and for the congregation, and pilgrims in the sense of vocation and purpose. Too often in the whole history of the Christian Church these essential elements have been separated from one another in a way that is certainly dysfunctional and probably heretical. Faith in Christ cut off from obedience and the fulfillment of his continuing ministry quickly grows introverted and irrelevant. A strong sense of vocation without a firm and continuing relationship to the source of one's identity in Christ becomes equally attentuated and ultimately is no longer a sign of the kingdom.

The present work of New York Theological Seminary, with its incredibly diverse student body, has offered a unique opportunity to explore ways in which these traditional dichotomies between piety and picketing, between the church as concentric and the church as excentric could be explored. For I am persuaded that whenever the church engages in internecine warfare, in bitter controversy between the different denominations or among those of different theological persuasion, it makes the victory of the forces of evil altogether too easy. In First Peter the author writes these striking words:

> Humble yourselves therefore under the mighty hand of God, that in due time he may exalt you. Cast all your anxieties on him, for he cares about you. Be sober, be watchful, your adversary the devil prowls around like a roaring lion, seeking some one to devour. Resist him, firm in your faith, knowing that the same experience of suffering is required from your brotherhood throughout the world. And after you have suffered a little while, the God of all grace, who has called you to his eternal glory in Christ, will himself restore, establish, and strengthen you. To him be the dominion for ever and ever. Amen. (I Peter 5:6-11)

When Christians use their energy to fight one another over such matters as the authority of the Scripture or the appropriate form, if any, for social action, then clearly the "devil" has an easy time. The diversity at New York Theological Seminary has revealed the fact that, particularly through the commitment and faith of brothers and sisters who come from Black Holiness and independent churches and also in the impressive Pentecostal movement among Hispanic congregations, there is a new possibility for unity in the church that transcends the old divisions which have been so disruptive of the unity of the Body of Christ. Again and again, Jesus Christ in his own words expresses the fact that the possibility of witness comes through our unity in him. Clearly our divisions, in whatever pattern they come, whether denominational, racial or class, disrupt our ability to see signs of shalom. I further want to emphasize the potential of overcoming the old familiar split between the "sect-type" of church organizations and the "church-type" by challenging our congregations to the discipline and commitment of the sect for the sake of identity, but with the commitment to public responsibility and social change that has been the style of the church-type.

Now I want to suggest how in three other critical areas usually marked by severe division we have a fascinating possibility for going beyond the old battle lines to a new unity of purpose that can bring together the most diverse Christian traditions in a community that recognizes diversity and pluralism without polarizing.

A. *Biblical authorship*. No controversy has been more bitter or prolonged in this century than the argument as to the composition and authority of the Bible. Heresy trials marked a heavy controversy between those who would defend the inerrancy and "verbal inspiration" of every word of the Bible against those who wanted firmly to establish the authority of the Scriptures but recognized that they had been composed over a long period of time under many different hands and could best be understood by what was called the methods of higher criticism.

This argument has continued to rage even in our own day, with a recent heavy attack on a conservative theological seminary by one of its former professors on the grounds that it had become too liberal in its biblical understanding and and really capitulated to the enemy. The result, as many readers may affirm, is that some people are prepared to defend the Bible by waving it wildly and proclaiming that they believe every single word in it. For them, it is the unalterable word of God. Thus, they make an idol out of the printed page when clearly the New Testment affirms that Jesus is the word of God and our ultimate loyalty is to him, not to a book. While those who stand on the conservative side have made an idol out of the Bible, those in the liberal tradition of higher criticism have tended to take the Bible completely away from the laity. The assumption quickly develops that trained scholars are essential for interpreting and understanding the Scriptures. Then hard-working parish clergy can hardly have sufficient skill and training to interpret the Bible legitimately. This wipes out the laity from significant participation in biblical study. No wonder then that the Bible has fallen on such hard days in our liberal churches. Many others find the whole controversy boring and irrelevant and opt for a high level of biblical illiteracy. They are among those who tried to read straight through and thus found Scriptures utterly confusing. More important, most Christian laity in congregations on one side or the other of the struggle are simply willing to accept the position of their own church and forget the whole controversy.

It is precisely at this point in history that the Pentecostal clergy and black pastors have brought a new insight to our life at New York Theological Seminary. Coming, as most of them do, from a conservative position on biblical authority, they have been quite eager to understand what this controversy was all about, to learn the arguments on the side of the higher critics. But they say quite simply that the argument doesn't cut much ice with them. The important matter, as far as they are concerned, is that their people really know the biblical story. For them, the important task is to be sure their people know the story of Abraham, Isaac, and Jacob; the great liberating acts of God in the freeing of the Hebrew people through Moses; the stories of the judges and the kings; of the great prophetic utterances; and above all of the whole New Testament witness to Jesus. As long as their people really know these stories and identify with them, they are not going to worry about the issues which have been so divisive in the past.

I am now persuaded that they really are on the right track. At New York Theological Seminary our professor of Biblical

Studies has been discovering, largely through the experience of black churches, that men and women from liberal mainline denominations can find a new excitement and power in the biblical tradition when they too learn the stories of faith and suddenly discover that they are illuminative of their own experience and provide a perspective on life that is authentic.

Our own faculty meets weekly for Bible study and has been forced to undergo something of this same rigorous discipline. As those almost uniformly trained in the traditions of higher scholarship, we are used to breaking down the passages into small segments and using all the resources that we have been provided by our scholarly mentors. The result is that we rarely look at a passage in its final biblical version. Because we are already using particular verses to make our own theological positions we often miss the important elements of the passage. When one is forced, literally, to the discipline of memorizing a whole story, one has to take seriously every word in that passage. Then powerful new insights emerge that have long been submerged through our over-familiarity with a particular passage. For us all, the old issue between those who hold to a fundamentalist, literalist interpretation and those who call for higher criticism has been quite transcended by a new discovery of the power and vitality of the biblical message when we are willing to take seriously what comes to us in the text in a serious grappling with the Scriptures, particularly in the context of a community where the Holy Spirit can get at us all.

B. *The church as spiritual community versus the church as a base for social action.* When our black and Hispanic clergy began coming to New York Theological Seminary in some numbers, we quickly discovered that the phrase "social gospel" was almost universally anathema. It had been equated with a vigorous engagement of the church in "worldly affairs," where, from their perspective, it really had no business. They had obviously been struggling very hard to help their people find a sense of identity and community in the life of the Christian community. They had to stand vigorously over against the oppressing forces of a city like New York but had little time or energy for fighting back. What is now striking, however, is that clergy from this background have been reading the history of the black community in the United States and liberation theology from the Third World. They are beginning to recognize that the problems which their people face and which have made it so necessary for the intense communities of faith to survive are forces of evil which can be named and against which they have a legitimate right to fight. A key has been the discovery of the important role of "principalities and powers" in the New Testament. When suddenly they realize that the board of education which betrays their children is a principality and power; that the criminal justice system, which is so unfair to people that are poor, is a principality and power; when they recognize that the medical delivery system in New York City is a principality and power, then suddenly there is a biblical mandate for action and responsibility. It brings a new unity between the necessity to picket and to pray.

In 1975, a group of pastors who had been in the College Program, sponsored by New York Theological Seminary, organized what is known as Accion Civica Evangelica. Within a year it was an organization of over 400 Pentecostal congregations and other Hispanic churches committed to public responsibility and willing to seek the welfare of the city through a variety of programs. In the fall of 1976, several Pentecostal churches on the lower East Side were burned out by vandals. Not a word appeared in the media. There was no attention given by the police in any serious way. Accion Civica organized a large protest meeting in the community and then, for the first time as far as I know, the Pentecostal churches in New York City actually marched in protest to the local precinct. The commanding officer spent a considerable amount of time with them, taking very seriously the fact that a powerful group of new community leaders was now suddenly on his doorstep. A leader of Accion Civica had hardly gotten back to his office at the seminary when he had a phone call from Mayor Beame personally assuring him that he would give serious attention to their problems in the future. This is not meant to be a success story, but it does indicate that when the Christian community discovers the resources of its own life in a new appropriation of the Bible, when new wineskins are found for the gospel, we can be signs of shalom even in a city as troubled as New York. As black and Hispanic clergy and congregations begin to cry aloud, they are a source of insight and challenge that fulfills in a very fresh way the mandate of prophecy and truth—telling that our world so desparately needs. It is no accident that Jeremiah 29:7, the verse we have been using throughout this book, has become an important source of insight for these congregations as they gratefully accept the insight of Jeremiah in placing together the need to seek the welfare of the city and to pray to the Lord on its behalf. The old dichotomy between praying and picketing can be overcome by authentic faith in action.

C. *Reform or Revolution.* Another source of striking disagreement that has enervated the churches over their history has been over the possibility and method for seeking social progress. A student in class the other day asked me whether I believed in progress through evolution on the one hand or did I believe that the Christian should be involved in some revolutionary action. The Hispanic and Pentecostal clergy have been deeply troubled by the vigorous language of liberation theology and by the involvement of many church persons in violent revolutionary struggles in Latin America and other parts of the world. Can a Christian rightly participate in such violence? They have sought some way of understanding where they belong on the spectrum from those who say the Christian should never participate in social action through those who have some simple belief that things are getting better to those involved in revolutionary struggles. Do they stand with those who believe that the kingdom will come in its own time and thus Christians need simply to survive until it arrives, or do they join those seeking to bring in the kingdom of God?

A community of exiles and pilgrims can resolve this dilemma by an altogether different commitment. We are revolutionaries, but for us the revolution has already happened. The Pentecostal and Holiness churches of New York City in many cases reflect a very dynamic style of life in which they seek now to live as those who are part of the kingdom of God. The discipline and participation required by their members reflect a serious attempt to understand and incorporate the words and patterns of Jesus' own life and ministry here and now over against the values of the culture of which they are a part. I have been impressed, for example, on the one hand by the drastic failure of the New York City Public School System to provide significant education for black and Hispanic young people and on the other hand by the young people who do manage to survive through that system and begin to achieve their own potential for effective living. Time and time again, the young people who manage to stand over against the powerful disintegrating forces of the educational system and, more important, the pressures of their own peers who feel no hope for significant achievement accomplish this by the strength and community which is provided by their participation in the storefront churches of this city. Here they find a community of peers and of adults who provide them with enough security and identity to survive in the educational institutions of the city. They are able to make use of the opportunities of the school system and triumph because of the secure base from which they operate. Against the pressures of our culture and particularly of their own peers this is a tremendous achievement

This is the critical power of the exile community. In seeing now with the eyes of faith the potent presence of the kingdom, in seeking ourselves to be signs of shalom, first fruits of that kingdom, we make a public witness that does not require us to create a revolution or judge our success by our ability to transform the society but does require us to be agents of God's kingdom within it. The word of the cross is a drastic change in our understanding of human history and the value of our lives. We place ourselves on the side of that revolution. We march now to the beat of a different drummer. That is to say, we are not involved in a bloody revolution to bring about social change, for we know that our revolution has happened.

That does demand that Christians stand with the oppressed and those bearing the scars from the principalities and powers who still are like roaring lions, seeking to devour us. For Christians in the United States it is thus possible to work for social change within the existing system in a style of opposition and resistance to that system. A different response may be required by Christians under varied political structures in other parts of the world. The principalities and powers in seeking to oppress us take different forms. I am grateful for the insights which have come from the black and Pentecostal churches that offer us a new opportunity to break through the traditional barricades that have divided the Christian community and dissipated our energies from the effective task of public involvement and witness. We are called to live with confidence in the faithfulness of God and in the hope that transcends our present suffering. As First Peter promises, "And after you have suffered a little while, the God of all grace, who has called you to his eternal glory in Christ, will himself restore, establish, and strengthen you."

We do live by hope. That is the only answer I know for that man in Richmond, Virginia, who challenged me as to how I could justify twenty-five years in the inner city when the visible signs around were of increasing problems and ever greater deterioration. Second Corinthians 4 is a refreshing source of insight and encouragement. It begins by reminding us that we have this ministry by the mercy of God and "therefore . . . do not lose heart." The phrase is repeated again in the verse 16: "So we do not lose heart." This, the New Testment affirms in spite of the fact that any sense of progress or simple optimism is impossible.

I am obviously setting the word "hope" over against the traditional use of optimism. Optimism means the confidence that if we work hard enough we can do something to improve the society, if not bring in the kingdom of God. Optimism is the confidence that if I am a good little Christian, God will bless me; it is the assurance of health and wealth in this present life. To be sure, that is a great deal of preaching in our day that offers this assurance to middle-class America. It promises that faithfulness to Christ guarantees the good life here and now. I find no such expectations in the New Testament at any point. Certainly, in the face of the manifest injustices of our own society, the issues we discussed of poverty, racism, sexism, and the demise of our cities, there is little hope for a better day ahead. As one reads over the terrifying words of the great Old Testament prophets and reflects on the situations in Israel to which they were addressed and then compares them to our own day, one can only tremble before the righteousness of God and wonder how he can resist bringing upon this nation the travails which we would seem so rightly to deserve. Optimism is impossible.

But pessimism is a cop-out. That is, we have no right either to retreat into personal escape, seeking only to take care of our own life in isolation from God's world, or simply to eat, drink, and be merry for tomorrow we die. Pessimism is a cop-out because the inaction or indifference of Christian men and women allows the forces of evil to hold sway with no challenge or check. Not to participate is always to participate on the side of the forces that are operative. For the Christian to be nonpolitical is to be highly political in the sense of firmly endorsing those who are in power. Pessimism is a cop-out.

Therefore, we live by hope, recognizing that we "have this treasure in earthen vessels, to show that the transcendent power belongs to God and not to us. We are afflicted in every way, but not crushed; perplexed, but not driven to despair; persecuted, but not forsaken; struck down, but not destroyed" (II Corinthians 4:7-9).

We do not lose heart because we know that God is faithful. Though we expect the battle to be tough and have no confidence that we will make things better, we have been blessed, all of us, by signs of shalom and encouragement along the way, by the support and strength of brothers and sisters in Christ who keep alive our assurance that whether we live or whether we die nothing can separate us from the love of God in Christ. This hope allows us to accept the reality of conflict without being either surprised or defeated. It is this hope which makes clear that God always takes his stand passionately and unconditionally on the side of the poor and oppressed against those who enjoy right and privilege. It is this necessity which means that the church must stand with the poor in love and service. It also has the right and responsibility to push the state in a similar direction. It means the Christian community is able to run the risk of involvement and compromise in the clear recognition that because we are earthen vessels we do not have to play God. We have the right to confess when we have with the best intentions made a tragic mess out of our efforts to love and serve our neighbor. When what we took to be cross-bearing turns out to be incompetence and stupidity, we dare confess to God and seek his strength anew for the continuing battle. Since we live by hope, we rejoice in the signs of shalom which we discover among people who do not even know the name of Christ. We give thanks when small signs of justice and reconciliation take place around us. We affirm and stand with them. Some years ago the Armstrong Circle Theater produced an hour show on TV about the work of the East Harlem Protestant Parish. The initial plan was to call the production "A Square Mile of Hell." Certainly, this would be an obvious description for any objective observer who looked at the terrible problems of that neighborhood. But we persuaded the producers to change it, since it was the story of God's people, to "A Square Mile of Hope." For in the midst of that hell of a community, there are signs of hope. That Christ is Lord of East Harlem and his people are present makes it possible for those with eyes of faith to see signs of the kingdom and to know that God never leaves us without the hope which gives life its meaning and its joy.